Katherine
wife of Luther

Katherine
wife of Luther

Clara Seuel Schreiber

Muhlenberg Press + Philadelphia

Third Printing

Library of Congress Catalog
Card Number 54-7588

Printed in U.S.A. *UB751*

To

H. W., Ruth, and Edgar

There is nothing lovelier on earth than a woman's love, if you can get it.

Ursula von Cotta

Chapter 1

It was the night before Easter, 1523. April starlight was obscured by flocks of roving clouds. Now and then a black mass would be caught on the horns of the slender, hooked moon, only to be swept onward the next moment.

A breeze carrying with it the earthy smell of awakening spring tore at dry vines that clung to the stone wall of the convent of Nimbschen near Grimma in the duchy of Saxony. In the uncertain light the building appeared spectral. Its windows were dark, as were those of the church, the dormitory, the refectory, and all the other buildings of the close. Even the house of the abbess was without light.

Now and then the moon peeped out at the rich, lovely valley. The surrounding orchards, fields, fishponds, vegetable gardens, and the beautiful wooded hills were convent property.

As it was Saturday night, all the usual activities had ceased with sunset. The mill which supplied the flour for the inmates of this aristocratic convent was silent. The great bakery ovens were cooling. No sound came from the smithy where the stalwart blacksmith always made sure all the hoofs of the work horses were in good order. The slaughterhouse from which so often the frantic clamoring of doomed sheep, pigs, cattle, and poultry could be heard was for once at rest. Most of the convent's many servants already lay stretched out on their straw pallets.

The clock in the church tower struck ten. Slowly a rear door of the convent opened. A shadowy figure slipped out, followed by another and then several others. Nine young nuns huddled against the damp, chill wall in tense silence.

"Katy," a frightened voice whispered, "don't you feel spooky?"

"Hush!" Katherine von Bora cautioned, "be calm, Elsie. Remember if we're caught we'll pay with our heads."

"Heaven forbid!" Elsie breathed fearfully. "Oh, Kate," she went on, "you're so brave. And yet you're only three years older than I—twenty-four."

"Are we all here?" asked Madeline von Staupitz in a hushed, resolute voice. She was twenty-eight, the oldest of the group. "Katy," she began to enumerate, "Elsie von Kanitz, Eva, two Zeschau sisters, two Schoenfelds, Loneta von Gohlis and . . ."

"And you, Madeline," Kate interrupted. "We're all here except the three who changed their minds at the last minute. I only hope good Master Koppe will soon get here."

"God help him," Madeline murmured. "He is risking his head to help us escape."

"What a saint he must be," Kate said. "But, of course,

everybody knows that he comes here regularly to deliver a barrel of beer or a keg of herring. The good abbess will be in the feathers by now. She won't smell the herring."

"Oh," Elsie cried softly, "do we have to crawl inside that old smelly wagon?"

"Of course. That is the only way we can hide. But listen! Yes, I hear something—wagon wheels, I think."

At the sound of rattling wheels coming closer, breathless excitement held their bodies rigid. Slowly and heavily the clumsy vehicle approached the entrance. There it came to a halt. Two men dismounted. They lifted back the heavy canvas covering and rolled out a barrel. In the glimmering moonlight Katy caught a glimpse of a slender, young figure and of a portly older one. Leonard Koppe, she thought.

"There," said a loud, gruff voice, "here's good Torgau beer for the abbess. Good Easter brew. Just to her liking."

"Yes, Uncle," replied the younger man, "it's a special Easter brew. How many empty kegs have we here?"

Elsie pinched Katy's arm. "Holy saints," she whispered, "they'll wake up everybody and then we'll be lost."

"Stop worrying," Kate said. "They know what they are doing. They have a purpose talking so loud. They want it to sound ordinary."

The men moved about in the dark, bumping against kegs and barrels. Suddenly Leonard Koppe flashed a light in the faces of the cowering nuns. "Come quick now," he mumbled softly, "crawl into the wagon. And don't mind the herring and beer smell. This means your freedom."

Freedom! What did they know about freedom after having been cooped up in the convent and subjected to its rigid rules since early childhood? Though all of the aristocracy, most of them had been brought here because they were orphans, or poor, or not wanted at home. All had been reared according to the strict rules of St. Bernard of Clairvaux. They arose early, prayed, chanted Matins in Latin, and kept the hours. What social contact they had with one another was by the abbess' permission or when they worked together. They could see visitors only through iron bars and were not permitted to accept gifts. Their day consisted of singing, praying, reading, writing, and studying Latin. The little leisure time they had was spent in doing fine needlework, such as embroidering cloth for mass robes and covers for the precious relics on the various altars.

While thus engaged they employed a sign language of their own or managed to communicate by secret whisperings. Now and then a word was dropped not meant for their ears. The cloister walls were not thick enough to keep out the reverberating thunder of momentous events in the world. They snatched up words like "great explorations," "new discoveries," "humanism and Erasmus," "Martin Luther" and "the growing unrest in the church."

Bit by bit Kate and a few of her intimates had gleaned facts about the audacious monk who had set the whole world aflame by posting his Ninety-five Theses on the door of the Castle Church at Wittenberg. That had been in 1517, when Luther was thirty-four years old and a doctor of theology at Wittenberg University. Kate knew that he had daringly denounced the celibacy of the clergy as well as the cloistering of nuns and monks. He had stormed against "indulgences" which were being sold everywhere at high church holidays and kermis.

No wonder Luther ranted. Kate herself would never forget how she and the other nuns, with priests, monks, magistrates, schoolmasters, and all the men and women of Grimma had marched to church in a grand procession. They carried torches and waved flags. They jingled bells, sang, and tooted horns. She remembered how the noisy crowd paraded into church to the burst of organ music. She had watched, wide-eyed, how the men had erected a large cross before the altar in the middle of the church. They hung the pope's silken banner over the cross and then dragged a huge, iron money chest in front of it.

Then followed a pious sermon, exhorting folks to buy indulgences for the remission of penalties for sins and for their soul's salvation. After that the drinking, dancing populace had given way to a night of pleasuring.

Kate had managed to get a word with the Zeschau sisters, whose brother was an Augustinian friar. She had seen the disgust in his face. He had given them to understand that "all good Christians were shocked at these doings." The "papists" were bleeding Germany. Luther was gaining friends and adherents. People sympathized with him for being excommunicated and admired him for publicly burning the papal bull. His valiant defense of his religious convictions at the Diet of Worms was the talk of the whole world. But now that he had been pronounced a heretic, anyone could apprehend him and kill him. He was in danger of being burned to death like John Huss. Kate fervently prayed that this would never happen to Martin Luther. Was he not personally assisting them to escape by sending his trusted friend, Leonard Koppe, here tonight? This information came from the Zeschaus, whose brother had now turned Evangelical. He, also, had sent them Luther's pamphlet "On Cloister Vows," which heartened the nuns to write to their relatives. Most of them, however, had not replied. Kate's brother, Hans von Bora, had ignored her plea for help. It was then that she and the Zeschaus had appealed to Luther, who had written to Koppe to contact Zeschau and inform the nuns of their planned rescue.

Master Koppe and his nephew mounted the high driver's seat of the clumsy vehicle. "Now, children," he said, half turning around, "not a sound out of you. No matter how many bumps you get or how you ache all over." Then he drove off with his unusual cargo.

Sighs of relief came up from the depth of the wagon box. Only Kate piped up, "Where will you take us, good Master Koppe? We have no homes."

Leonard Koppe flipped the reins and clucked with his tongue. "Where else," he said, "but to Doctor Martin? Is he not to blame for all this running away? But," he added significantly, "I think he will find husbands and homes for all of you."

So saying, he unfolded two heavy robes and tossed them into the wagon box. "Better cover up," he said, "this spring air is cold. And we ride all night."

As they snuggled under the covers, Elsie nudged Kate. "Husbands?" she whispered, awed. "Do we have to get married?"

"Of course," Kate whispered back, amused at Elsie's naivete. "What else would you do? Pray God to find you a good, honest man, and give you good children." She did not hear Elsie's reply. She could easily imagine that she was covering her eyes in shocked silence.

The wagon rattled on, now splashing through mud puddles, now bumping over rough, half-frozen ground, again scraping over rocky surfaces. The passengers maintained a deathlike silence throughout the night. In their cramped positions, with the chill night air congealing their blood, the uncertainty of the future weighted them down. The fear of being apprehended made the hours of the night drag out endlessly as they crouched among the beer barrels and herring kegs.

Elsie roused Kate from the heavy sleep into which she had finally fallen. "Look, Kate," she whispered, shivering with cold and excitement, "it is getting light."

Kate blinked. "Thank God!" she breathed fervently. "We're free! We're miles from the convent and in the good Elector's free territory."

Master Koppe just then turned and shouted into the wagon, "We're going to cross the bridge and then we'll be in Torgau! That's where they make that good strong beer the abbess likes so well."

The abbess! The word made the inmates of the wagon come to life. "Yes, the abbess!" they whispered, "what will she say? Easter morning and nine good, pious nuns missing from Matins."

Day was just breaking. Roosters crowed. Birds chirped. The bell of St. Mary's Church began ringing as if to greet the refugees. Kate gazed with fascinated eyes at this new world beginning to unfold before them. Their wagon rumbled into the yard of the parsonage. Pastor Zwilling, a little man, stumbled out of the house.

"Thank God!" he exclaimed excitedly, "it's done. Bring them in, Koppe. My sister will give them hot barley soup."

Without much ado the women climbed out of their cramped quarters and moved into the house. "Saints," Kate murmured, "surely we can't stay here, good Master Koppe. Where—"

"Come, come!" Zwilling urged impatiently, "in with you! No noise, no commotion! Even though you are now free. These are serious times. Madeline will tell you what to do."

Kate immediately liked good, motherly Madeline, who was ladling out the steaming soup for them. How good the warmth of the house felt this chilly spring morning! How they relished the hot barley soup!

"Now, girls," Madeline cheered, "have courage. You are free and all will turn out for the best. God has led you here, and there are many good, worthy men anxious to wed you."

"Anxious to wed us?" Elsie repeated. "Us . . . poor lonely nuns?"

"Tut, tut! You are free from the vows you were forced

to take. Free to marry and go where you will. Our good Dr. Luther says so."

"Oh, if Dr. Luther says so," Kate quickly cried, "then I believe it. I believe every word he says."

"I, too," Elsie nodded. "And I," said Margaret von Staupitz. "I will thank the dear God on my knees if he brings me a good and honorable man for a husband."

"Yes," the others agreed quickly, "that is the best thing that can happen to us."

"But how can we meet any men?" Elsie asked innocently. "We can't go anywhere with our cropped heads. And we have no fine clothes, no decent shoes, and not even one groschen to our name."

Madeline patted her shoulder. "God will provide," she intoned softly. "You are all fine-looking damsels and of good health. And God has brought you so far. Surely He will help further."

"Well!" Kate's head went up. "We can earn a good dress and maybe a few florins now that we are free. When we look more presentable and have more hair on our heads, men won't be so afraid of us." Kate had a proud way about her. Though not handsome, her even features, the flashing blue eyes, the animation with which her whole face lighted up when she spoke, made her attractive. She was quick and outspoken. Now, glancing at Madeline, she detected a faint smile on that motherly woman's face as she replied reassuringly, "Even so, dear child, they won't be afraid of you. You are all cheerful, of good homes and good character—anyone can see that."

"I wonder," Kate said, "how long it takes to earn a florin. I can't wait to get rid of this mourning gown!"

Suppressed giggling answered her. In spite of their rigorous upbringing, they could not hide their amusement. Even old Madeline smiled faintly.

"Truly, Kate," she said, "with your spirit and your energy, I think they will have to find a big, important man for you. Maybe a merchant would make a good husband."

Kate shrugged and looked at Elsie, who sighed.

"Why so sad, little one? Now you can let your golden hair grow long and show your pretty face. Are you not glad we're free?"

"Certainly." Elsie brushed a tear from her eyes. "But it's always 'a man' and 'marry.' Is there nothing a woman can do without a man? I'm afraid of men. They're rough and hard."

"Come," Madeline interposed, "this is idle talk and not fitting to young women brought up like you. Go to your rooms now. Get ready for church. Tuesday, Master Koppe has promised to drive you to Wittenberg." Then, as they slowly filed out of the big kitchen she put a detaining hand on Elsie who was last, "Dear child, don't worry so much about being afraid of men. When the time comes, you will feel different. God has just as many good men as good women in this world."

Elsie gratefully caught her hand and kissed it. "I will remember that," she said, brightening.

Pastor Zwilling breezed through the kitchen at that moment on his way to church. "Madeline," he said solemnly, "see that these children come to the service. Afterward they can enjoy the day."

She promised and with a nod at her charges reminded them to be ready when the bell began ringing. To Kate it seemed a triumphal march as they walked to the church in pairs. They held themselves demurely, unaccustomed as yet to this freedom. The curious eyes of the whole congregation seemed to be centering upon them. Never in their lives had these young nuns sung the glorious old Latin Easter hymn so wholeheartedly:

Christ is arisen
From the grave's dark prison.
We now rejoice with gladness,
Christ will end all sadness—
Hallelujah! Hallelujah!

Over and over they sang it that day.

"Tomorrow," Kate said, "will be Easter Monday. And on Tuesday, Master Koppe will drive us to Wittenberg."

"And we shall meet that great man of whom we've heard, Dr. Martin Luther."

"Yes," Kate agreed. "I can hardly wait to see him. We owe our freedom to him."

Chapter 2

They went to church in a group on Easter Monday and again sang "Hallelujah." The rest of the day they spent helping Madeline. They ventured but a few steps out of the yard, conversing in low voices and wondering what the morning would bring. Although they were in free territory and the people appeared friendly, this new freedom was still too overwhelming to be fully comprehended.

Tuesday morning dawned at last. It was still early when faithful Master Koppe drove into the yard with his big wagon. Kate was the first outside to greet him. While they waited for the others, she took notice of his two beautiful, brown horses.

"Master Koppe," she remarked, stroking the animals' heads, "what fine horses you have! They seem to understand everything you say to them."

Koppe nodded. "Yes," he agreed thoughtfully, "I think they do. They are like children," he added, "they want to be loved and cared for."

"I love horses," Kate commented, as the other young women joined them and all clambered into the wagon. "I love all animals. And children, too."

Koppe smiled approvingly as they rumbled out of the yard. Kate sighed. Now they were off to Wittenberg to meet the man the whole world was talking about. All along the way they kept curious eyes on the countryside. Earth was awakening from its long winter sleep. The air was bracing. Leaves showed in many trees. Birds twittered and sang. After several hours' jogging they reached Wittenberg. How great was their amazement to find crowds of people standing in the streets waiting to greet them! Windows and doors were jammed with onlookers who smiled and waved. Groups stood about the famous old Castle Church, where Luther had posted his Ninety-five Theses. As the wagonload of maidens craning their necks drove by, the townspeople cheered again and again. Students gathered about the University noisily clapped hands. At the market place they were hailed as heroines.

"Holy saints," Kate whispered excitedly, "the whole town's out to greet us! They must all be Luther people here."

"Looks like a good start for our new life," Elsie remarked.

"But not a good town," Eva von Grosse put in drily. "Why, it's all mud and sand. Thank God, my brother will call for me and take me away from here."

"Well," Kate sighed, "I'm not so lucky. I may have to stay here. I have no one in the world except my brother, Hans, who failed me."

"If you do stay," advised one of the Schoenfeld sisters, "don't get into a rut. I see nothing of culture in this place. Look at those small, ugly houses!"

"And the streets are so narrow," criticized her sister. "I wouldn't live here for any man!"

"But don't forget the University," Kate reminded them. "There must be learned men here. Think of Dr. Luther —and Master Philip Melanchthon. Lucas Cranach, the great painter, also lives here."

The Schoenfeld sisters turned up their noses. Eva von Grosse looked away and Elsie said, "How can they ever stand to live in such a marshy place? And how could Elector Frederick start a university here?"

Eva said something about "an unhealthy place to live." Kate heard no more. Her attention was centered on the scene before them. They were entering Black Cloister premises. She held her breath. What a huge building! How it seemed to frown upon its badly neglected grounds! She felt awed as well as thrilled. The thought of seeing Dr. Martin Luther face to face gave her a nervous feeling in her stomach.

Koppe turned halfway around and, pointing with his whip, said, "See, that's it—the Black Cloister. People are waiting for you here, too. Oh, I see the good Doctor just coming out! That man close on his heels is Wolf Sieberger, his man-of-all-work. Poor Wolf tried to study at first but always flunked."

Kate had a feeling of weakness as they neared the building. "Heaven help us," she whispered to Elsie, "the doctor surely can't mean to pen us up in this awful place!" Aloud, she asked, "Do they call it Black Cloister, Master Koppe, because it looks so black and forbidding?"

Koppe burst into laughter. "No, no," he assured her,

"it will not always look so 'black.' Soon the old pear tree yonder will be loaded with white blossoms. It never fails. And the lilacs on the other side where the Elbe River flows will be in bloom." He paused, then went on, "The young monks that used to dwell here were robed in deep black and hence the name—Black Cloister."

Kate felt too tense to smile just then. A quick glance at her companions assured her that they were just as anxious as she herself was. They all sat bolt upright as the wagon came to a halt in front of the wide cloister entrance. Kate noted at once that the arched door was even with the ground floor. She reasoned absently that it must lead into the tall adjoining tower with its diagonal windows. The building itself must be bright on sunny days for it was studded with windows—bay windows on the second floor, tiny cell windows on the third floor, and a number of dormers on the roof.

Neither building nor windows however, could long hold Kate's attention at this time. She had immediately singled out one man among the group that stood waiting there. Luther! She could not take her eyes off him. She had expected to see an emaciated, fire-eating monk. Instead, she saw a typical university doctor, wearing the customary long coat over his doublet and hose. A white collar fitted snugly around his neck. A black beret covered his head and the dark curls that peeped out from under it intrigued Kate.

His rugged face wore a grave expression. Every feature from the heavy jowl to the broad forehead, the fleshy, stubby nose, and the firmly shut mouth denoted strength.

Dauntless courage, great sincerity, unshakable faith were indelibly stamped on that physiognomy. And those dark, burning eyes! Kate thought she saw a twinkle in them as Luther turned to Koppe to shake hands.

"Well done, good Leonard," he said in an agreeable tenor voice, "just unload your poor orphans at my door. I shall write and publish a letter, explaining the right they have to be free. This will exonerate you from all guilt. I will shoulder all responsibility."

Kate felt her heart go out to him with great warmth. She wanted to say something, but Elsie nudged her, "How kind he looks! Not like a big thundercloud. Never would I have dreamed that so great a man could be so human."

Kate whispered back, "I already respect him. But . . . how much he must have suffered!" She was the first to dismount and shake hands with Luther. The others followed, one by one. He greeted the "orphans" cordially.

"You are all welcome to stay here with me in this big house," he said cheerily, "until God provides homes for you. I usually have a houseful of refugees. But there is always more room. Of course, you will have to take things as you find them. There's no one to cook or keep house except my famulus, Wolf."

While he was speaking an elderly, courtly man approached and addressed him. They conversed for several minutes, now and then casting glances at the group of young women. Then Luther asked, "Are there two Schoenfeld sisters here?"

When the sisters stepped forward, he took their arms and led them to the courtly stranger. "This is your uncle," he said. "He has come to get you. And . . ." he added, an unmistakable twinkle in his eyes, "he thinks he has already found two suitable husbands for you."

The sisters blushed, bowed, and exchanged greetings with their uncle. Elsie pinched Kate. "Look how red their faces are! Why are they hurrying so?" she added, as the two hastily made the rounds and kissed their friends goodbye.

"They are glad to go to a real home," Kate murmured.

When they had gone, Koppe also took his departure. Luther opened the wide, arched door and led the way into his cloister home. "The Zeschau sisters," he announced, preceding them up the circular stairs, "will probably be called for by their brother tomorrow. He has turned his back on monkery, as you know, and has been given a pastorate near by. He will provide for them. Madeline von Staupitz," giving her a nod of recognition, "your brother has sent word that he will come for you—tomorrow. The others," he added thoughtfully, looking at Kate, Elsie, Loneta and Eva von Grosse, "will have to wait until we can find places for them. The good Elector has promised to help. He will send food and clothes. He knows that the beggar's bag always has a hole in it." They had reached the top of the stairway. "Here," he said, preceding them into the large, bare room, "you are welcome to make yourselves at home as best you can."

They could not find words to thank him. They could only smile gratefully and tearfully.

"Doctor," Eva von Grosse spoke up, "I will only be here till tomorrow. My brother will come for me."

"Good, good," Luther nodded. Then, seeing how hard Elsie was struggling to hide her tears, he approached her and put his hand on her shoulder. "You, my child," he said in a brotherly way, "have you no one at all? You look too young and innocent to be out in this world alone."

Elsie shook her head. She swallowed hard. She tried but could not speak. "In Grimma," she faltered, "a friend . . . perhaps," she added, ever so shyly, "I could teach in the new girls' school if you . . . would help me."

Luther patted her arm. "We shall see. Put your trust in the good God." With a parting word, he turned and walked away.

When he was gone, Elsie burst out, "Oh, what a soul shines in those eyes!"

"They are like firebrands," Kate observed. "They look right through you." She took Elsie's arm and led her to the bay window. "Look! there is the pear tree Koppe mentioned. And the lilac is ready to burst open. How sweet it must smell here then! I tell you if I had a place like this, I'd make something of it."

"You would," Elsie murmured, "even if no one else could."

Chapter 3

Kate and Elsie soon found comfortable quarters with Philip and Margaret Reichenbach, young newlyweds, who lived in a large house near St. Mary's Church.

A few days after Eva had left the Black Cloister and gone home with her brother, taking Loneta with her, Luther brought the invitation to Kate. He told her that Philip Reichenbach was a promising lawyer and, at this time, city clerk of Wittenberg. His wife was a young woman of excellent family. She was anxious to have Kate stay with them as long as she liked. Elsie, of course, was to go with her and stay until the girls' school in Grimma notified her. She was deliriously happy when the summons came a few weeks later.

The days passed pleasantly for Kate. She and Margaret Reichenbach became close friends. Kate realized that here she was getting a course in housekeeping which she could not have gotten elsewhere. Margaret nicknamed her a "model of industry." The students, frequenting St. Mary's, noticed her exemplary behavior and dubbed her "Catherine of Siena."

Margaret introduced Kate to many prominent Wittenbergers. Among these was Philip Melanchthon, the youngest professor at the University. Kate marveled at the superior knowledge of this young man, about her own age, whose brilliance of mind was recognized even by the great Erasmus. Melanchthon's sensitive, almost feminine features and his extremely shy manner were in direct contrast with Luther's virility. In spite of this and a difference of fifteen years in their ages, the two men were close friends. Melanchthon's wife Katherine, whose father had been burgomaster of Wittenberg, was a daughter of the rich *bourgeoisie.* Although the friendship between the two women was only lukewarm, Katherine invited Kate to the social evenings in the Melanchthon home.

Kate was only too glad to take advantage of this invitation, for here she often met Luther as well as students and intellectuals. One of the students was Jerome Baumgartner from Nuremberg. His gay, carefree manner, the friendly look in his blue eyes, the courtesy and attention he showed her, charmed Kate. She soon confided to Margaret that she was in love with Jerome and Jerome with her.

They were seen together more and more frequently. Jerome openly courted Kate during that first year of her stay in Wittenberg. Luther voiced his approval of the match. Everyone expected that the romance would culminate in marriage. When Jerome left for his home at the end of the term, Kate had his promise that he would send for her soon so that they could be married in Nuremberg.

Then Kate waited to hear. A week passed without a sign of life from Jerome—two weeks. Soon it was a month, then two months. Still not a word from him. She began to feel nettled. People looked at her wonderingly. Her pride was stung.

When Jerome did not return to school in the fall, Margaret playfully asked Kate one lovely October evening as they walked in the garden, "And when are you and Jerome planning to marry?"

Kate shook her head. "Never."

"But he asked you to marry him before he left, I thought."

Kate was hesitant. "He did," she murmured in a low voice, "but it's all over. Maybe his parents objected to his marrying a poor nun. They're well-to-do, you know."

"Kate," Margaret cried warmly, "you're no longer a 'poor' nun. You are a housekeeping woman with a record for efficiency. Well—" she shrugged, "if he can't even write you a word, he isn't worthy of you. And I—"

"Oh, don't worry," Kate forced a gay laugh. "To me Jerome's a thing of the past. And it isn't good to regret the past."

"There are others," Margaret pursued. "Seems to me you have many admirers."

Kate shrugged indifferently, thankful for the growing darkness that hid her face. She hoped the subject would never again come up. What was her dismay, therefore, several weeks later when she met Luther and he accosted her teasingly, "When do I get my invitation to the wedding?"

"Wedding?" she repeated. "What wedding?"

"Why, yours and Jerome's."

Kate averted her face for a moment. Then she turned toward him resolutely. "Don't you know, Doctor, that there will be no wedding?"

"What! And why not?"

"Because he has not written me once. He has deserted me."

"Why, the unfaithful rascal. I shall write and find out why."

He did. But it was not until months later, when Kate had discarded all thought of the affair, that Luther told her he had heard from Jerome Baumgartner. The letter sounded apologetic, explaining his marriage in January to the girl of his parents' choice. And that was all.

It was more than enough for Kate. Other things occupied her mind. She had received a letter from Elsie, telling her that all the nuns had left the convent. Elector Frederick did nothing to hinder or punish them. No one cared when the abbess herself had deserted and taken Kate's Aunt Lena with her. The convent was closed now, as were many others, for everywhere monks and nuns were seeking their freedom.

When Kate told Luther this he expressed no surprise. "It is everyone's Christian freedom," he explained, "to follow the dictates of his conscience. I teach nothing new. I have only unearthed the precious jewel—justification by faith—so long buried." He cleared his voice and hesitated a moment before speaking again. "Your youthful romance has shipwrecked," he said slowly. "God did not wish you to marry Baumgartner. You have had almost a year to forget him. And there is one, right now, who would like to marry you. He has said as much to me. He could well support you, being a respected doctor at the University."

A deep red colored Kate's face. "You mean Dr. Caspar Glatz," she shot at him, unable to hide her displeasure.

"Yes." Luther regarded her with surprise. "Why are you so disturbed about this?"

Kate shrugged impatiently. "If you knew," she retorted, "how Glatz pursues me with his sanctimonious looks every time we meet at Melanchthons—if you could see that expression in his eyes and the way he tries to get close to me! Ugh! Just the touch of his clammy hand gives me a chill."

He shook his head sadly. "Kate," he said, "you sound uncharitable. Could it be true that you are plagued with pride—ancestral pride?"

She hung her head. "Yes," she mumbled guiltily, "it could be. But that has nothing to do with Glatz."

She knew that Luther went away unconvinced. Perhaps he thought her not only proud but also stubborn. When she told Margaret Reichenbach about this talk and mentioned her dislike for Glatz, Margaret seemed just as surprised as Luther had been.

"But, Kate," she argued, "you should feel honored to have a doctor at the University woo you."

Kate replied with that characteristic toss of her head that made people think her proud, "But I do just loathe his holiest of holy talk. Yet his eyes speak so different a language that I can't help but distrust him."

"Oh, Kate! surely that can't be true. What would Luther say if . . ."

"I don't care what he says. In fact, I've already told him how I feel about Glatz. Rather will I be husbandless the rest of my life!"

That settled it. Kate was a determined individual. To avoid further meetings with Glatz, she went more frequently to the Lucas Cranach home. A mutual liking already existed between her and motherly Barbara Cranach, the master's wife. Both were many years older and treated her like a young sister. Master Cranach, a stocky man with a heavily bearded face, was goodheartedness personified. He spent most of his time painting portraits and teaching his young son the art. Barbara helped him in the small printshop and pharmacy which he also owned.

Luther often came here, Kate soon discovered, for Lucas Cranach was one of his closest friends. The master always liked to get Luther's opinion of his portraits. When he displayed his most recent picture of Frederick, the good Elector of Saxony, Kate was thrilled. She studied the broad, bearded face which so exactly resembled that of his brother John. Both wore large floppy berets and displayed fine white, lace-edged shirts under their heavily furred coats.

Here, too, for the first time Kate saw a likeness of the great Erasmus. At the Melanchthon gatherings she had heard enough about him to arouse her curiosity. Some said that Luther's bold stand frightened the timid scholar.

He believed that Luther disturbed the peace. As Kate stood gazing at him among his books, his body swathed in a voluminous, wide-sleeved gown, his ascetic face almost hidden by his hood, she wondered whether he would ever take a definite stand.

Back at Reichenbachs, Kate discussed all these matters with Margaret, who was as interested as she herself was. They were sewing and chatting one winter evening when Barbara Cranach surprised them by bursting into the room excitedly.

"Think of it," she announced, "King Christian of Denmark is coming to our house. Lucas had a message from him today asking to stay until he can settle his affairs."

"Is he in trouble?" Margaret asked. "What has he done that he should be driven from his country like that?"

Barbara shrugged. "One hears conflicting things about him. Evidently he's not a saint, but Lucas thinks we should not refuse his request."

"M'm," Margaret commented, untangling her yarn, "how thrilling to have a king sleep in your house."

"I should say!" Kate's eyes sparkled as she spoke. "I'd like to see King Christian of Denmark."

"You may," Barbara assured her. Then, looking at Margaret, she added, "At least, I hope . . . if Margaret lets you."

"And why shouldn't she?" Kate asked pertly.

Barbara cleared her throat and played with her fingers. "That's why I came over tonight," she explained. "Margaret, will you loan Kate to me while the King is with us? You see, I want to have everything just as nice as I can and Kate knows all about fine things. I can set a nice table for my own use but, after all, I haven't that instinct for royalty that Kate was born with." She looked so pleadingly from Margaret to Kate that both began to laugh.

"Why, of course, I'll gladly let you have Kate if she so wishes."

Kate agreed to go with Barbara then and there. But she felt like turning back when they entered Cranach's house and her startled eyes fell upon Dr. Luther. He greeted her in his usual cheery way. His talk was so impersonal and so animated that she soon felt she had nothing to fear. It was strange, however, this pulling at her heartstrings every time she saw him. She wondered now whether it was her motherless childhood and his harsh youth that seemed to draw her to him so strongly.

As Luther turned to go, Lucas Cranach said, "Wait a minute. I want to show you something." He disappeared behind his studio door and came back carrying a portrait.

"Look, Doctor, what do you think of this?"

Luther took the picture and examined it with great interest. "Why, it's Kate," he commented, looking from the painting to the young woman before him. "And you have painted her as quite a fine lady, Master Cranach. Never have I seen her look like this. Yet—it shows well her heavy blond hair, her blue eyes, and her comely face. But what finery and frills!"

"Well," Barbara put in quickly, "Kate has just been outfitted as she deserves to be. Now she will be presentable when King Christian comes to our house."

He looked surprised. "Oh, then the King is really coming and Kate is going to meet him?"

"Not only meet him," Cranach laughed. "She is to supervise everything. My Barbara is afraid she might be embarrassed."

Luther nodded. "No doubt," he said, "Kate will do you great honor. I wish you well." He moved toward the door. Then, seeing that the master and his wife were going out and that Kate was still standing there, he said, "Dr. Glatz has been asking about you again. Are you still against marrying him?"

Kate's head went up. Angry tears filled her eyes. With all her reverence for Luther, she felt that she must, once for all, set the great, naive man right.

"Dear Doctor Luther," she pleaded, a deep red flooding her face, "I am quite sure that I do not wish to marry him. I will never change my mind about him."

"So determined," he said playfully. "I should think a damsel like you without family would welcome marriage. You know," he added, quite soberly, "God made woman to depend on man. A woman alone in this world is without protection."

Kate nodded. She already knew it. She had experienced the loneliness of belonging to no one. Her brother and sister, whom she barely knew, paid no attention to her. They were such impoverished aristocrats that they could not trouble about her.

Luther said no more. He bade her a friendly good night and went out. Kate did not see him again to speak to for over a month. Meanwhile King Christian had come and gone. He had visited Luther and had been impressed by him. He had presented Kate with a ring which she treasured highly. In spite of all this excitement she could not forget Luther's last visit. Somehow she felt that she had not convinced him of her intense dislike of Glatz. She had not made it strong enough. She must do something to prove to him that she was not merely stubborn or ungrateful, but that she felt a positive physical aversion to Glatz.

The thing so worried her that one evening while still busy in the kitchen after Barbara had gone out, she did her thinking aloud. "He must be displeased with me," she murmured, "because he never comes. If I could only see him and tell him. But Amsdorf is in town now and he is his best friend. If I could . . ." she paused, a faraway look coming into her eyes. Suddenly her hand came down on the table with a bang. "I'll do it!" she said emphatically at the very moment Barbara returned, carrying her youngest child under her arm.

"Kate," she laughed, "are you daydreaming? Or with whom do you hold conversation?"

Kate dropped a heavy kettle and, quickly picking it up, sighed, "I do not know, Barbara, I was only thinking."

"As long as you were not thinking of Jerome Baumgartner. He . . ."

"No! No! I have long ago forgotten him. Isn't it almost two years since that silly infatuation? Remember I am twenty-six now and much more sensible. He does not interest me any longer since he's married another."

"And Glatz?"

"Oh, Barbara, please, don't you know that the last time the good Doctor was here he again asked me about him?"

Barbara looked up, surprised to see angry tears in Kate's eyes. "But, my dear," she pursued, "why are you so against marriage?"

Kate raised the hem of her apron and touched it to her eyes. "If the right one comes," she replied slowly, "and asks me, I will be glad to give him my hand. But not before that."

"Well," Barbara soothed, "we are only too glad to have you stay with us longer. And Margaret wants you back, also."

The next day when the early evening meal was over, the table cleared, and the children in bed, Kate quietly slipped out. Resolutely she set her face in the direction of the Black Cloister to see Amsdorf. He would be there. He was still visiting Luther. This was Kate's chance. Tonight Luther would be preaching to the students in the tumble-down, near-by chapel. If she hurried she need not fear meeting him.

She drew her cloak closer against the damp, raw March air. The streets were dark. In spite of the small lantern she carried, she had literally to grope her way to the cloister. Luckily, she had learned her way around Wittenberg during the two years she had been here. She suddenly remembered what the Schoenfeld sisters had said about the ugly little town with the muddy streets.

A dog startled her. She had not noticed him until she felt something at her heels. No doubt he was investigating her personality by means of his nose. She gave him a swift push. Obediently he disappeared. A stray cat mewed wistfully. Kate lifted her lantern but saw no cat. Thank God, she was almost there. If she had much farther to go, she might weaken and give up. When she took hold of the knocker at the door to announce her presence, her heart beat so uncontrollably that she thought Amsdorf must hear it as he came to open the door.

"What brings you here this raw spring night?" he asked, inviting her in, in spite of his shocked surprise. "If it's Doctor . . ."

"No! No!" Kate quickly interrupted, following him inside and up the circular stairway into Luther's study. She sat down gingerly in the chair he proffered. "It is you I came to see."

Amsdorf brushed his hand over his eyes as if he were trying to erase a nightmare. "Me?" he asked.

Kate felt herself getting hot and cold all over. Now that she must speak, she trembled. Her tongue felt dry. How rash of her to come! How unbecoming of a young, unmarried woman to enter this domain of men! To sit here in the great Doctor's private study.

"Well," she hedged, fumbling with the buttons of her cloak and pushing back her hood, "I had to come." She swallowed hard, looked down, rubbed her fingers together nervously and looked up at him. Suddenly she pursed her lips and burst out, "I have a favor to ask you, Dr. Amsdorf—something of which I can speak to no one else." She swallowed again but, seeing that he was listening with calmness and sympathy she went on, less flustered, "Every time I see Dr. Luther he plagues me about getting married to . . . Dr. Glatz."

Amsdorf nodded gravely. "And why don't you?"

Instantly her nervousness left her as she shot back, "Because I do not love him—and never will!"

"And what am I to do about it?"

"You are to tell Dr. Luther to please leave me alone!" she blurted out heatedly. "I hate the very name, Glatz, by now."

Amsdorf appeared perturbed. "Then you are absolutely opposed to marrying?" he queried wonderingly.

She rose and moved to the door which he opened for her. "N-no . . ." she said with downcast eyes. "Not if the right one asks me."

She caught a glint of amusement in his eyes as he pursued quickly, "The right one! And who might that be?"

Kate was halfway down the winding stairway. She turned back to face him when she reached the threshold. "It must be a man of strong character," she said rapidly, "like Dr. Martin Luther. I'd marry him any day. Or at least a man I could look up to—like yourself. But Glatz! Never!" With a slam of the door she was gone, stumbling along the rough uneven footway.

For two weeks she saw Luther only on the Sunday he preached in the Castle Church. Again a feeling of deep admiration welled up in her heart. She had the same sensation a few days later when she came into the house from an errand and found Luther sitting there, chatting with the Cranachs.

He gave her a friendly nod. "Well, young lady, how does the weather suit you?"

"It's cold," Kate said. "But soon it will be April and the lilacs will come out and the apple trees will bloom."

"And also my old pear tree. Ah," he murmured, "I could make a paradise of that old garden with the Elbe rolling by and whispering stories at night."

"Doctor," laughed Lucas Cranach, "you are an artist and a poet as well. You should not work at such hard matters as reform. Come, Barbara," he said, taking her hand, "you were going to help me in the shop. Let Kate entertain the doctor tonight."

"By all means," Luther said, with a gesture of his hand, "do what you planned to do." Then, turning to Kate he added heartily, "A fine man, this Master Cranach and a fine wife to help him."

"Yes," Kate agreed. "They have made me feel much at home with them. But Margaret Reichenbach wants me to come back to her."

Luther nodded and for several moments seemed lost in deep thought. Suddenly he looked at her with an expression in his face that startled her. "Kate," he said softly, "how would you like to come to the Black Cloister as my wife and live with me for the rest of your life?"

Kate swallowed. It was too overwhelming. Marry Dr. Luther—this great, most wonderful of all men, whom even Erasmus revered, and the like of whom God had not sent into the world since Moses! True, she had impulsively mentioned his name to Amsdorf, never thinking that it might become a reality. No, no. It could not be true. She must be dreaming.

Seeing her confusion he caught her hand and pressed it warmly. "Kate, I will love you and honor you as a husband should. I have a deep warm feeling for you, but I am not madly in love. Could you take me under those conditions, remembering also that they who persecute me might end my life suddenly?"

Kate felt his warm, strong clasp. Hot tears filled her eyes. Twice she tried but could not speak. At last she said modestly, "I am honored more than any woman in the world. Yes, I will be glad to be your wedded wife. And I do love you and respect you with all my heart!"

Chapter 4

Kate was in high spirits. She went about the house singing. She hugged the children whenever she could get hold of one.

Thoughts buzzed through her head like swarms of bees. She had been reproved for being proud, yet now she could not help feeling proud indeed! The most talked-of man in all Europe, the man who had set the world afire, had asked her to be his wife.

She loved this man, Luther, although she knew that half of the people in the world hated and reviled him. Princes and high churchmen wanted to see him burned to death or beheaded.

Kate had no fear of this. God would protect her Doctor, for He still had work for him to do. Had not God protected him mightily on that dangerous journey to Worms in 1521 where he was asked to defend his cause before the highest assemblage in Europe?

Resolutely he had told his worrying friends: "Though there were as many devils in Worms as tiles on the housetops, I will none the less enter there." When pressed to recant, he had said: "Here I stand. I cannot do otherwise. God help me. Amen."

No wonder Kate had thought him a giant among men ever since she heard the first whisperings about him in the convent. She knew that the storm that followed his bold stand in Worms had driven his frightened friends to kidnap Luther and whisk him off to the Wartburg fortress. Here he had remained for months, disguised as "Squire George," translating the New Testament. When fanatics caused disturbances in Wittenberg, he hurried back to teach and preach. Later, when he had helped the "poor orphans" to escape from their convent prison, assuring them that freedom was their God-given right, she had revered him. This feeling had deepened with each personal contact until it became love.

Although Luther had cautioned Kate to keep their engagement quiet, she had let Margaret and Barbara into the secret. They would help her sew a suitable dress and embroider a few fine linens for the new household. They could be trusted not to spread the news. The times were troublous. Besides there were many other things to worry about. The nobles were no longer safe in the country since the peasants had begun to rebel against them.

Lucas Cranach declared one chilly spring morning, as he came into the room where the three women sat sewing, "Everywhere there is rioting. The peasants are burning the castles and convents, plundering the noblemen's homes and roaming the country like wild animals."

The women shuddered. "Have any been killed?" Barbara asked.

"More than we know. I hear they are armed with pitchforks and axes. They stop at nothing, especially those led by that archfiend, Thomas Muenzer, who commands them 'in the name of God' to stab, kill, burn, destroy whatever is in their way."

Kate's face paled. "Luther," she asked, suddenly afraid, "where is he? I have not seen him for many days."

Cranach patted her shoulder. "Do not worry, child. God will protect him as heretofore. Luther is on a perilous journey preaching against this mob rule. He has stood in the midst of the murderous rabble and denounced their actions. He has tried to explain that freedom of conscience does not mean license or disobedience to authorized governments."

Margaret Reichenbach sighed deeply. "They hate the well-to-do merchants also. Many a time did my father express fear that these things would happen."

"It all began," Barbara said, "when Luther was in the Wartburg and the radicals stormed the churches and tore down pictures and altars."

There was a knock at the door. When Cranach opened it, Luther himself entered. Kate immediately ran to him. "Oh, my Doctor," she cried, looking into his haggard face, "how tired and worn you look! You need rest, clean clothes, and good hot food."

Barbara Cranach nodded, put down her sewing basket and immediately left for the kitchen. Luther sat down heavily. "The peasants are losing everywhere. Already the princes are arming and putting them down with brutal force. Both are guilty of atrocities. We must pray," he added gravely.

Barbara returned at this point and invited Luther to the kitchen for a bowl of hot barley soup and a cup of warm beer.

Kate was close at his heels. "And Elector Frederick?" she whispered. "Heard you about him?"

"He died early this morning and I am to preach the funeral sermon day after tomorrow in the Castle Church."

"Then I will go to hear you," Kate promised.

She was happy when Luther told her later that John, the new Elector, would follow in his brother's footsteps. He was deeply interested in Luther's cause and eager to see it progress.

Now that the uprising was calming down, Luther seemed less heavyhearted. The beautiful May weather lifted his spirits. He told Kate that his beloved pear tree had burst into bloom overnight. The lilacs were opening, too. The old convent garden with all its wild growth was enchanting. Kate could hardly restrain her impatience. She would transform it as she had told Elsie.

The time was closer than she realized. One evening early in June, Luther startled her by asking, "Kate, could you be ready to marry me in a day or two?"

"Why, Doctor?"

"I think we should marry without delay. It is not good to talk much about such matters. A man must ask God for counsel, and pray, and then act accordingly."

Kate agreed and asked, "What day have you in mind?"

"I have decided that the best day for me is Tuesday, June 13, after the Feast of Trinity. Can you be ready by then?"

Kate promised and he left, looking happier than he had for many weeks.

On the appointed evening Barbara Cranach helped Kate dress. Carefully she combed her heavy blond hair. After parting it in the center and bringing it straight back, she wound it around Kate's head in a coil. Then she placed a silver snood, her own personal gift to Kate, over it all to hold it in place. This done she brought out the dress of fine white material. It was heavily embroidered at the waist and hem. The long puffy sleeves were also embroidered. Barbara arranged the lace ruching at the neck and handed her the lacy half-gloves and dainty handkerchief given to her by Margaret Reichenbach.

Lucas Cranach and his wife went with Kate to the Black Cloister which was henceforth to be her home. At the door they were received by the bridegroom dressed in a mantle of fine, dark cloth from which peeped his white neckband. His new shiny boots showed under his gown and on his head he wore the customary velvet professor's beret. He bade the Cranachs be seated and said to Kate, "I have asked a few friends over for the civil ceremony." Bugenhagen, who represented the Town Church, was first to arrive. Justus Jonas, pastor of the Castle Church, was next. Apel, professor of law at the University, who himself had married a nun, brought the written contract.

Before Bugenhagen began the actual ceremony, Luther addressed them solemnly, "Friends, I know that many, even my friends, will not approve of this act. But," he sighed and went on, "when I wanted to wed my Kate, I prayed to God with all earnestness. I am convinced that our marriage is pleasing to Him."

When Bugenhagen asked Luther whether he would take Katherine von Bora as his wedded wife, he responded with a firm, "I do." And when he questioned Kate, her reply came unwaveringly. Thereupon Dr. Apel told them to join their right hands and pronounced them husband and wife in the name of the Triune God. There was a moment of deep silence. When Kate looked up she saw tears in Jonas' eyes. Luther drew her close and said, "This is my wife with whom I shall now celebrate our marriage."

The following day when Luther suggested to his wife that they celebrate their wedding publicly on June 27, with a service in the Town Church and a reception afterward she readily agreed. Nothing could have pleased her better. Even though she had lost contact with her own family and friends it would show the world how they felt about their marriage. Nothing secret about it. Let everybody come and see.

The first invitation went to Luther's aging parents, whose fervent wish had always been that their son might marry. A few intimate friends from Mansfeld were invited also. To Leonard Koppe, the good old hero of the Easter Eve escapade, Luther wrote, "God has suddenly and unexpectedly caught me with the band of holy wedlock . . ." Kate was deeply touched by these words. She, herself, had still not gotten over the wonder of it: a homeless orphan and former nun married to Martin Luther, doctor at the University, theologian, writer, preacher, and himself a former monk. Truly, God must lead and guide the destinies of men. Already people were whispering, Barbara said—friend and foe alike. It was too new, too unheard of! They could not understand what the reaction would be. Surely Luther was harming his cause by getting married.

Even Philip Melanchthon had opposed this marriage bitterly. In a letter written to a friend he called Kate "conceited and proud." She knew also that he had expressed "terrible shock" at this marriage. Luther had told her that there were others who shared Philip's idea. Oh, well, they would probably all change their minds some time, she thought. She would not let it worry her so long as she could live for her beloved Doctor. Besides, had not Luther declared openly that he merely put into practice what he was preaching—that the clergy should feel free to marry?

June 27 dawned brilliantly. Kate rose early. She went about opening windows and doors, inhaling the fragrant air. A burst of bird music greeted her. She stood enchanted for a moment. Then, as she surveyed the great living-room with its heavily carved furniture and woodwork, the high ceiling, the pine floor, the deep window niches with small leaded panes, and the immense cupboard with so little in it, she shook her head.

"It will take much planning," she murmured, "and it will take money to change this into a cozy family room.

That window niche," she mused, "will be just the right place to sit with my sewing."

Walking across the bare floor, she stood before the long table where the wedding guests would dine, inspecting the homespun linen cloth that covered it. It was a gift from Barbara. Dear Barbara! It was she and Margaret Reichenbach with their servants who were roasting the venison sent by the new Elector for the occasion. They had taken upon themselves the responsibility for the entire wedding dinner—fish, fowl, pork and venison; great loaves of bread; sweets and fruit. The city had sent wine. There would be beer, too, of course.

Footsteps roused Kate from her thoughts. "Doctor," she cried, going to meet him. He kissed her lightly. Then, fumbling in the folds of his gown he produced two rings. "Here, Kate," he said, fitting one on her finger and the other on his own, "our rings. A friend had them made for me."

Kate couldn't resist examining them. Hers had a ruby with the initials C.V.B. His had a diamond with the initials M.L.D. Then she reached into her pocket and, blushing, handed him a ring. "This, Doctor, is my pledge to you."

He took it and seeing on it the crucified Saviour, said thoughtfully, "Thank you, dear Kate, for choosing this ring. Always it will represent what I preach and pray—Christ crucified. And it is He in whose name our marriage will today be confirmed."

She nodded, took his arm and left the room with him to get ready for the church service. When this was over, the wedding guests proceeded to the Black Cloister in a long line. The reception was followed by the wedding dinner at eleven. Luther's aged parents were seated at the head of the table. Then according to their rank: Spalatin, the Elector's secretary; Jonas, pastor of the Castle Church; Bugenhagen, pastor of the Town Church; Amsdorf, friends from Mansfeld, Koppe, professors, and others. Kate could not name them all until much later. The Cranachs, the Reichenbachs, and the Melanchthons, of course, were old friends. She looked across the table at the Melanchthons. Philip had become reconciled to the marriage by now. But she wondered whatever could have induced him to write such a "nasty" letter. He looked happy, but why did Katherine seem so "different." It was nice, though, to see with what reverence her Doctor treated his parents. He kissed them, escorted them to the table and himself seated his mother. He was not ashamed of them, of their calloused hands, their wrinkled faces, their brown complexions, and their pinched, severe features. How he honored them!

"Look, Kate," Luther said, "there is my brother Peter, about whom I've told you."

Kate was delighted to meet her husband's youngest brother. They made a place for him at the table and Kate asked him how long he thought he could stay with them. He explained that he would have to return with his parents. Then, across the table, Kate's attention was attracted by Leonard Koppe. She would never forget how much she owed him.

"Master Koppe," she exclaimed, "how glad I am you came!"

"Ah, yes," he laughed in his hearty way, laying aside his chunk of dark bread, "it is good to see you, Mrs. Luther. Whoever would have thought that when first we met?"

Kate nodded and replied jestingly. Looking in another direction she caught Amsdorf's eye and blushed. Could he be thinking of that evening when she had unburdened her heart to him and so impulsively remarked that she would marry Martin Luther if he asked her? To be sure, the significant look in his eyes made her think so. Later, as she passed him in leaving the table, he murmured, "It's a great day. And it will come to mean much in the world. May God give you happiness."

As Kate and her Doctor moved on she caught a glimpse of Lucas Cranach and Bugenhagen. They were conversing with the old Luthers, whose ascetic faces had assumed a certain soft look of happiness. Peter had left the table and was now standing in the window niche behind them. As he stood there beside the fur-coated, bearded Cranach, now listening to the master, now beaming at the famous brother he hardly knew, Kate found she liked him. How much he resembled her Doctor. His nut-brown hair flowed freely about his face. His bright blue eyes followed the goings-on with rapt attention. His eyes met Kate's several times. Each time, Peter smiled broadly at his new sister-in-law. At last Kate spied Barbara Cranach sitting in that beautifully carved, old, oak chair. She had been watching Kate, an expression of dreamy contentment on her comely face. She looked tired but happy.

"Kate," she called softly, "Lucas is going to paint a wedding picture of you two." When Kate seemed surprised, she added with a smile, "It would be nice to have our little flower girls with their baskets and the wreaths on their heads. The blossoms strewn on the floor would look pretty in the picture, too. But Lucas will know what's best."

Kate expressed her appreciation and her great joy at everything and remarked, "I think that Doctor would like to have a picture of his parents."

Barbara smiled. "That is what he was talking to them about just before. They were a little hesitant."

Kate pointed to the smaller table before she went on to rejoin her husband. "I see that Margaret is still busy with the servants. I hope she joins us soon. It looks as if they're getting ready for music," she added. "I see a flute, a lute, and a viol there. The director is looking over his music."

"Katy Jonas will like that," laughed Barbara. "You know she loves to dance. She's so gay."

Kate was about to say something when suddenly her Doctor grasped her hand and pulled her forward. Elector John had sent a messenger bearing his congratulations as well as the news of a doubled income. He went on to say that the cloister was to be Dr. Luther's own home, tax-free, as long as he and his wife lived. Another messenger bore the congratulations of the University in the form of a tall, silver, loving cup. There were messages from the town council. Others bore gifts of pewter, purple cloth, linens, towels, goblets, and kitchen articles. While they were looking and listening a stranger pressed forward. He held up to view a fine Venetian glass. Among all the gifts they received, including three handsome clocks, Kate thought this was the most exquisite. In her enthusiasm she exclaimed delightedly, "Oh, how very beautiful that glass is! Do you see, Doctor?"

"Yes, Kate," he nodded, "I see. And I see, too, that it is much too fine for our use. So I will give it to a friend of mine who can really use it."

Kate felt such a lump rise in her throat that she found it hard to speak. "But it was given to us," she protested.

"It would tend to make us too worldly, my dear Kate."

She swallowed hard. Speech failed her. Just then she glanced up and saw Justus Jonas' eyes fixed on her. Evidently he understood her distress, for he gave her an encouraging nod and, pointing at the glass, snatched it up, let it disappear in the folds of his mantle, and turned to go. His adroitness brought a smile to Kate's face. When Luther called after him, "I'll want that back very soon," she merely sighed happily.

She forgot about it presently when a representative of Prince Albert of Brandenburg stepped forward and handed her a package. Eagerly she opened it, exclaiming naively, "Oh, Doctor, look at this twenty gulden! It's just what I can use for the house."

He put his hand over hers and gently removed it. "No, Kate, I can't let you accept it."

"Why not?"

"Because Prince Albert is a man with whom I have had unpleasant contact. I have no reason to believe that he is my friend."

"But that doesn't mean I can't have the money," Kate countered.

"You are my wife, Kate, and everything you do reflects on me."

Kate could not hide her disappointment. "Oh, Doctor," she frowned, "why turn everything down and give everything to others? Don't you realize how badly we need money to make this place livable? You have nothing! I have nothing! And still . . ." Her mouth quivered. Tears started to her eyes.

"God will provide," he maintained firmly.

She was quick to catch her cue. "God can't provide," she said, looking straight into those burning, brown eyes that awed so many people, "if you toss away what God provides. Do you think He'll hand you another twenty gulden?"

Her reasoning broke down his resistance. He placed the package back in her hand, squeezed it shut and held it tight. "You are right, my Kate," he admitted. "God gave the gulden for you to use for the new household."

Overwhelmed, Kate bent down and kissed his hand. "Thank you, my dear, kind Doctor. Look," she added, pointing at a group of guests, "they are getting ready to sing."

One of the professors had the people move closer together. The director gave the signal to the musicians and singers. They began with folk songs and ended with an ancient melody, "All praise to Thee, Jesus Christ." After saying the Lord's Prayer in unison, the wedding party came to an end.

Altogether, Kate reflected, as she helped her aged parents-in-law to their room and then retired to her own, it had been the happiest day of her life. A long time after, she heard her Doctor come. Before getting into bed he stood before the window, looking out into the dark, starlit night, speaking to God.

Chapter 5

Kate was up at dawn the next morning. Luther was still sleeping, and she was careful not to waken him. She must help him with the burdens of his strenuous life. There was much she did not yet know about him, she realized, although he had told her about his youth as a miner's son. The family's poverty was so great that his mother was forced to go out into the forest to gather sticks of wood for fuel. He had told Kate of his stern upbringing. He had related how his beloved mother once chastised him so severely for taking a nut that it drew blood. He had told Kate of his school life, of tyrannical teachers, and of earning his daily bread in Eisenach by singing in front of people's houses. Here Widow Cotta heard him and took him into her home as a dear, adopted son. He loved to speak of his "dear Eisenach," and of all he had learned in this fine, patrician home. It was Ursula Cotta, too, who told him, "There is nothing lovelier on earth than a woman's love, if you can get it." He spoke of his fasting and starving, his tormented and agonized life in the cloister. Nowhere could he find peace of mind, for Christ was pictured as a stern and cruel judge. He spoke with affection of his old monastic superior, Dr. Staupitz, who had comforted him under the pear tree when his tormented soul was at the breaking point. Staupitz had taught him, "For peace with God he must look not to his own good deeds, but to the redemption of Christ." After Luther found the Bible passage, "The just shall live by faith," his soul became serene.

Kate told him the little she knew about her childhood: how her mother had died when she was an infant and her father had placed her in a "home" till she was five years old. Then she was brought to Nimbschen, where she had been till the escape.

Kate thought of these things as she slipped into her voluminous skirt, brushed her blond hair back, pulled her coif over it, and proceeded noiselessly into the big living-room. Every trace of yesterday's wedding celebration had been cleared away. Here was home, Kate thought, a smile warming her face. Her home and her Doctor's home.

It wasn't much of a home as yet, but she would make it one. For one thing the timbered ceiling was attractive. She would put her best dishes on the plate rail, and plants on the window sill. Yes, the room could be made very livable. All it needed was a woman's touch. A spinning wheel, for instance, in that niche opposite the immense five-tier stove from Nuremberg. She took a step closer to get a better look at the stove. It was made of green tile. The tile had pictures of the four Evangelists on it. To Kate the stove was a wonderful creation. She was glad, however, to know that she would not need to take care of it. Wolf had been in charge of the great stove for the last eight years. He would tend to the heating as usual.

Kate sighed. To be given such a great, sprawling building with only the crudest furnishings on your wedding day was unusual. Originally built as a dormitory, the building had forty cells for monks on the third floor. All these cubicles she intended to convert into livable little rooms for guests, boarders, and transients. She foresaw that she would always have a houseful. This living-room on the second floor was going to be her favorite spot. Beside it and the master bedroom there were four other rooms which faced north and looked out on the yard. On the opposite side were the lecture and recreation rooms that faced the Elbe. The Doctor's private study was in the tower. A door separated it from the living-room and another door led through the circular stairway to the ground floor.

Kate started down thoughtfully. This lower, basement floor was in a deplorable condition. Part of it was used for cooking. Tubs and vats stood around. The old blackened utensils made her shudder. The refectory was not much better. Everything was worn out. The old brick fireplace where most of the cooking was done had already been lighted by Wolf. Smoke was making its way out through a hole in the wall several feet from the ground. But there was enough escaping smoke to make her cough and blink. She took a quick look at a black kettle squatting on the brick, half filled with barley and water, and turned away. Wolf had also brought in water for drinking. On the table stood a bowl of garden-fresh strawberries.

She was more interested in the plans she was contemplating than in the strawberries. First of all, she wanted a decent kitchen with new, clean utensils, then, a storeroom where winter vegetables and dried fruits and other things could be stored. She wanted a laundry. She would need a servants' room or two. She could foresee that such a large and growing household as this promised to be could not be run without help. Later on, she would . . .

"Kate!" Footsteps sounded on the stairway.

"Good morning, Doctor," she greeted him.

"So busy already," he teased. "Early in the morning—plotting against me?"

"Tsk, tsk!" Kate shook her head. "As if I would ever plot against you, Doctor. No, I was merely looking things over to see what needs to be done. I have thirty gulden, you know."

"Ah, yes," he sighed, "you did manage to keep the gulden. Is that the way you'll always use your arts and wiles to win me over?"

Kate laughed. "If it becomes necessary." Then, sobering, she said, "I don't know what to give you for breakfast. Wolf was here ahead of me and started a fire and put some barley in the pot. I'll look at it."

She crossed over to the fireplace and looked into the steaming pot. "The barley soup is about ready," she announced. She ladled some into one of the tin dishes, took a few slices of thick bread and a pat of butter from a cupboard and put it before him on one of the small tables.

"Sit down, my Kate," he said, "we will eat together and pray together."

They folded their hands while he spoke a prayer. When the meager breakfast was finished, he rose saying, "I haven't much time, Kate. As you know, lectures begin at seven. Work is pressing."

"You'll be back for dinner at ten, as usual?"

He nodded. "Yes. And there'll be several students, maybe a professor or two, some theologian or other visitor with me. And you can usually count on Philip, too."

"Yes, Doctor. I'm beginning to learn that. There is someone at the door right now."

He went to answer the knock, and admitted a pale, thin-looking student. "And what can I do for you?" he asked cheerily.

The young student coughed and nervously played with the cap in his hands. "Good Doctor," he began timidly, "you help so many. Could you spare me a small coin?"

Quick sympathy showed in Luther's face. But he shook his head. "I'm afraid," he said, "that I'm broke myself." He felt in all the pockets of his gown and, finding nothing, turned to look for something. Suddenly his eyes fell on the silver goblet given him by a friend as a wedding gift. It was still standing on the shelf where he had left it.

Instantly, too, Kate looked at it. Their eyes met. Hers were strongly disapproving. She frowned and made as if to snatch the goblet up, while the mendicant stood as if hypnotized. Then Luther's arm shot out ahead of his wife's. He picked up the goblet, pressed it into the stranger's hands and said, "Take it. It is worth money if you sell it to the goldsmith. Use that money for your needs."

Profuse thanks and then the man was gone, and Luther with him. Kate stood alone. Angry at first, she muttered, "He'll give the very shirt from his body. What does he think we'll have left to live on? Well," with a toss of her head, "surely he must know. He always tells me 'God is a rich Father. He has many more silver goblets.' " She brushed a rebellious tear from her eye.

She soon forgot about the goblet. There was so much work to be done that she hardly knew where to begin. The entire building was in need of repair and thorough cleaning. The ground floor, first of all, should be whitewashed. Perhaps Wolf could do that.

"Well," she mused, starting up the winding stairway and stopping for a peep at the living-room, "what I need most of all up here in this large room is a wardrobe from Nuremberg to store my good linens and clothes. Also, chairs and benches."

She surveyed the room a moment, then continued up to the third story for her first good look at it. Some of the rooms facing south were being occupied at present by students. Each had in it a straw pallet, a chair, a small table, and shabby, inadequate bedcovers. She resolved then and there not to rest until every bare cell was converted into a habitable room. As she opened one of the small windows a fresh smell from the river blew in. On her way down she paused a moment in her Doctor's private study. For a while she stood dreamily at the window watching the broad Elbe flow by and inhaling the fresh air.

"A Herculean task," she said, descending slowly, "is confronting me. Thank God, I'm young and strong. But now I'll have to find something for dinner. First of all, I'd better run to the market place."

But it wasn't necessary. For there in the great living-room sat Barbara Cranach waiting for her. She lifted the cover of a huge market basket, saying, "Kate, I knew you'd be short of supplies, so I brought you a head of cabbage and a piece of pork and some smoked sausages for dinner. Here's a loaf of bread, too."

"Oh, Barbara," Kate cried, throwing herself into her old friend's arms, "it must be true, as my good Doctor says, that God will provide!"

Barbara nodded seriously. "Yes, Kate, I believe that."

Kate released her hold and wiped her eyes. "But this is so strange, dear Barbara. This morning, when we have nothing in the house but a few leftovers from yesterday, a poor student comes and my Doctor gives him a silver goblet, one of our wedding gifts, because he has no money to give him and . . ." tears again stood in Kate's eyes.

"And you were a bit angry?" Barbara suggested tactfully. "Kate, don't ever let little things like that make you interfere with Doctor Luther's goodness of heart. He is a saint . . ."

"Yes, yes, I know," Kate was half laughing, half crying. "I don't want to, Barbara. But I am so human, so small, so closefisted and my Doctor is so—so big."

Barbara looked into her starry eyes. "Kate, then you do really love him?" she asked softly.

"Yes," Kate's head dropped. "With all my heart."

"Oh, then you will work together," Barbara said, picking up her basket. "And all will come out well. Then," she added, backing to the door, "do everything for him, be everything to him, Kate. But don't be a door mat. Even God does not want women to be so humbled."

Kate was suddenly herself again. "I can be humble wherever Doctor Luther is concerned. But otherwise it's hard for me to subdue my proud spirit."

"I know," Barbara said, "that you're humble with him. But not with others. They're still saying that you're proud." She picked up her basket. "I suppose," she suggested, "that you'll want the pork and the sausage and the cabbage downstairs where you can cook it."

Kate nodded. "The bread can stay here on the table," she said, following Barbara downstairs. "And thank you once more."

Barbara turned back, calling, "God be with you," and hurried away. Left alone, Kate began to cut up the cabbage. "This and the sausages," she told herself, "will make a fine dinner with the beer left over from yesterday. And there's enough for ten—though I hope there won't be that many today."

She looked up quickly when the door opened and Wolf came limping in. Kate did not feel that she knew this gaunt leatherskin well. Doctor had told her, however, to make Wolf help her. He was perfectly trustworthy, although a bit indolent and slipshod. He had originally come to Wittenberg to study but, failing in everything and having no family ties, he had attached himself to Luther.

"Good morning, Wolf," Kate said. "Will you help me with the fire and bring in more wood?"

Wolf doffed his cap respectfully. "Certainly," he said politely. He took the poker and began stirring the fire so that smoke, sparks, and ashes spread all around. Then he put a huge chunk of wood into the fire. Going to the table he picked up the bowl of strawberries. "Did you see these?" he beamed. "I found them in a corner of the garden."

Kate smiled approvingly. "That's just what I need for dessert. I'm so glad you found them, Wolf."

He helped her in his slow way so that, by ten o'clock when Luther appeared, she had the dinner ready. With him came Philip Melanchthon and Conrad Cordatus, an Austrian refugee of Hussite parentage who had been taken in by Luther. Several students followed.

"Well, Kate," Luther called gaily, "have you a bite for us hungry beggars?"

"More than a bite," Kate replied proudly. "I have cooked cabbage and good, smoked sausages—the ones you like so much. And there's beer to drink with it and plenty of bread and butter. And strawberries which Wolf found."

Luther stared. "What," he asked, chucking her under the chin, "can it be that you are a witch? Look, Philip, what my Kate has for dinner."

Melanchthon's ascetic face brightened as he got a whiff of the steaming food. Maybe he would actually eat, Kate thought, as she placed the bowls on the table.

"Come now, Doctor," she urged. "Don't delay. A hot dinner must be eaten hot."

They stood at their places at the table. When Luther gave the signal, all folded their hands while he said grace. Then all sat down, Melanchthon and Cordatus at his right, Kate at his left. Wolf was at the other end of the table and the students in between.

"I must say," Luther said, after the first mouthful, "my new wife is a good cook. Excellent sausage—this."

"Oh," Kate intercepted, "I didn't make that, Doctor. Barbara Cranach brought it this morning. "But," she added proudly, "I helped her make it in March."

Luther nodded. "I know, Kate. Well," he went on, "there's a story connected with sausage. I think Philip knows, but Kate has never heard it. Have you, Cordatus?"

The one addressed shook his head. Kate saw him take writing materials from his garment and fasten expectant eyes on the great Doctor.

"When I was a boy," Luther began, "you know how poor my parents were. I had to make the rounds singing in front of houses for my bread. Others, too. So one day we happened out in the country, thinking the farmers would surely have something to spare. I remember it was getting a little dark and we were already uneasy. Suddenly the kitchen door was flung open, a dog jumped out and a man in a terrible voice roared at us, 'Hey, you rascals . . .' We dropped everything and tore away helter-skelter. The man pursued us. Then one of the boys fell and we had a revelation. The coarse voice pleaded, 'Boys, stop running. I have some sausages for you.' How we laughed as we thanked him!"

Cordatus put away his notes. "That is an interesting story," he remarked. "You must have many more."

"Many," Luther agreed. "But they can wait for another time. Time presses. And now that we have enjoyed this good food from the Lord's bounty, let us give thanks to Him for it."

All rose while he spoke the prayer, then the men dispersed. Luther and his "dearest Philip" started for his private study in the tower where they would be busy translating the Bible for the rest of the afternoon. Bugenhagen and the venerable Cruciger appeared while Kate was still clearing the table. A little later two other scholars, Aurogallus and Roerer, came to help also. They were having an especially difficult time right now with Job. "We have so much trouble," Luther had told Kate. "Job seems to be much more impatient of our efforts to turn him into German than he was of the consolation of his friends." And Kate knew that they had been laboring on three lines these past four days.

Well, her job right now was to "translate" her Doctor's bed. She would have to get Wolf to help her carry out the straw sack and feather mattress on which he slept. The crisscross ropes which served as a spring could not be removed. With an armful of pillows and covers, she was on her way out to hang them up for airing and at the same time look for Wolf.

"Mrs. Luther!" That wasn't his voice. It was old Hannah, the Reichenbach's servant. "I came to help you," she said. "Mrs. Reichenbach said you'd have more than you could do alone."

Kate nodded soberly. In the early days, while she was with the Reichenbachs, she had always wondered why she so often had wanted to laugh when she looked at Hannah. Now, suddenly she knew. Hannah's habitually open mouth with its vertical lines at the corners gave the impression of a perpetual grin. Kate had a genuine liking for her, but one had to get used to a face like that, she thought.

"Ah," she exclaimed, "here comes Wolf to help us carry the bedding down. The feather bed will be first." They helped pack the unwieldy thing on Wolf's shoulder and he slouched off with it.

"Oh," Hannah gasped, "surely Doctor Luther doesn't sleep under feathers in summer."

"Of course not."

Kate laughed hard. Then with arms akimbo and her hands on her hips, she stood looking at the servant critically.

"Hannah," she asked, looking serious, "what would you do if you married a man over forty who had lived alone for many years and was always too busy and tired to make his bed?"

"Saints alive!" Hannah exclaimed. "Did no one ever make his bed all these years?"

Kate's face assumed a solemn expression. "No. No, his bed was never made. He just fell into it at night. He had too many cares, too many things to think of. There was not a soul to bother about him."

Hannah crossed herself and then shrank under Kate's disapproving eyes. "Is it sin," she asked quickly, "to cross yourself?"

"Not if you do it with a prayer in your heart. But if you keep doing it all day long without really meaning it, then it's like taking the Lord's name in vain."

"How smart you are," Hannah remarked, as they went inside to get the other bedding. "No wonder he married you. Did you learn all that in the convent?"

"Not that. But I learned many things in the convent which I could never have learned elsewhere, and for which I am truly thankful."

Hannah clasped her hands above her heart. Again Kate laughed. "Well, Hannah," throwing a few covers and quilts over her arm, "let's take down the rest of the things. There isn't much of anything in this house, but this winter I'll get busy making quilts."

About three o'clock their work was interrupted by a messenger from the Elector with a mess of fish. Hannah helped clean the fish. Later, she brought in the well-aired bedclothes. "I will be here again tomorrow," she said as she left for home. "I'm to help you every day until you have a servant of your own."

Kate suppressed a little sniff. She wanted to say "There'll never be a servant here because there'll never be money to pay one." Instead, she said quietly, "I don't know, Hannah, the good Doctor gives everything away."

Kate had supper ready by five. There was a heaping platter of fried fish, bread, golden butter, honey, milk, and another bowl of berries that Wolf had brought in.

"Well," Kate greeted the weary scholars as they struggled in, wiping their damp faces, "how was Job this afternoon?"

Luther laughed heartily. "It takes all of us to get one little word out of him. He sits there and won't budge."

In the quiet of the evening as they went arm in arm to look at their garden, a wilderness, and stood watching the quietly flowing Elbe, Kate said suddenly, "Doctor, we have much to do. I want to make a real garden here—flowers, vegetables, berries, and fruit. And later, I hope to get chickens and . . ."

"Everything," he laughed, catching her in a warm embrace. "Certainly, Kate. Everything within reason. And Wolf shall help you. And I'll help you."

"How good of you to say that!"

"Kate," he said softly, "I think God specially reserved you for me. I wouldn't give you up for a kingdom. I love you more every day!" And Kate hid her face on his shoulder and sniffed happily.

Chapter 6

Kate had cleaned house to her heart's content. Assisted by Hannah, who kept right on coming, pay or no pay, she had chased the dust out and driven the moths from the remotest corner. From the once cheerless cells on the third floor to the ancient fireplace on the ground floor, everything had assumed a new look.

Even though she had been unable to carry out all her plans for a separate kitchen, storeroom, laundry, and bathroom, at least the walls were freshly whitewashed. The old refectory did not know itself. The Black Cloister was beginning to look like a home.

Luther said, "Kate, you are wonderful."

"At least I got rid of that old worm-eaten, moth-infested chest in the living-room," Kate rejoiced. "I had Wolf burn it. And I'm proud of the new one from Nuremberg."

"Master Kate," he jested, "only you could have inaugurated this cleaning jubilee and seen it through. Now, what is next?"

"The garden," she was quick to say, "and the entire grounds look like a jungle. I think they are full of snakes and toads and lizards."

"And what do you propose to do, good Master Kate?"

She ignored this surprising nickname the second time. "Why, plow it, dig it, cultivate it, and get it ready for spring planting. I've already mentioned it to Wolf."

"Wolf?" he burst out laughing. "If you can make a farmer out of Wolf, then you can do more than I can. Wolf doesn't like to exert himself. He believes in taking things easy."

"Well . . ." Kate was uncertain for a moment. Then she quickly brightened. "There are farmers all around Wittenberg. Surely one would do this for us."

"With pay," he replied significantly.

"Of course. Didn't the Elector just double your salary? And didn't he give his permission for me to charge thirty gulden per year for each boarder like the other professors' wives?"

"That's like a drop in the bucket," he said. "Now that I'm married, more people come here than ever before—for meals, for lodging, for money."

Kate's eyes suddenly flashed. Her Doctor's indiscriminate generosity was still a sore spot with her.

"No wonder we have nothing!" she flared. "You give everything away and will take nothing for your work."

"I have a rich God."

"Oh, yes. But what does the rich God say if you give it all to worthless beggars and cheats?"

"Kate, I will not commercialize my preaching and lecturing. I preach and write for nothing, in contempt of the world, that it must see one can do good because one is a Christian."

She shrugged, unconvinced. She needed money so badly for so many things, and it was a long time before next year's garden crop would bring in anything.

"If you would only take what you rightfully earn," she murmured, a bit resentfully. "Think of the valuable mining stock the Elector offered you for translating the Bible. And Philip would give you 1,000 gulden for translating Aesop into German."

"Yes, and I could get 100 gulden a year from Hans Lufft for printing my writings."

"Oh, Doctor! And you will not take that, either?"

"Kate," he put his hand on her shoulder and looked straight into her eyes, "there are other values." He said gently, "God does not look at the money we have or could have. He has His own measurements."

When she still seemed downcast, he chucked her under the chin. "Look, Kate, how rich we are! We have each other and we have a merciful, forgiving God. Kate, you know not what riches are in that assurance! To be at peace with God—to have a good conscience!"

Kate hung her head and said it must be that she was mercenary. Or, was it after all the too persistent, too incessant need for money that haunted her? How else could she get the pots, the pans, the kettles, the bowls for the kitchen? How about money for the hemp, yarn, linens, wool, not to speak of the daily needs for living?

She thought she had the answer to this, at least, in part, when one morning a young doctor came to her door. He had been sent by Bishop Lang of Salzburg with a gift of twenty florins. Kate invited him in and, as she quickly considered her great needs, accepted the money with thanks. What was her horrified surprise, when the young man mentioned it to her Doctor at the dinner table, to see him glance at her as if displeased. He came to her immediately, looking unusually stern.

"Kate, I want you to give back those twenty florins to Bishop Lang of Salzburg."

"Oh, Doctor!" She was plainly nettled. "How can I? What will he think?"

"Makes no difference, Kate. I will not let you accept that money. There is no excuse for it. Will you get it at once?"

She ran off in a huff and, coming back, tossed it at him just as Philip Melanchthon came in.

"Well!" he said, looking from one to the other.

"Well!" Luther said, looking extremely unhappy. He sighed deeply. "Philip," he said, "Kate is angry with me. However, if I have stood God's wrath for so many years, I think I'll be able to bear my wife's displeasure for a short time. Come, Philip," he added sadly, "the translating must go on. And I must find that man from Salzburg."

They went out, leaving Kate to herself. She was trying to collect her thoughts and beginning to cool when Hannah surprised her by coming from the ground floor.

"Was Doctor Luther mad?" she asked, a commiserating grin on her face.

"No!" Kate's answer was abrupt. She brushed her hand across her eyes. For once Hannah did not make her feel like laughing. The incident had completely upset her. Was she always going to be humiliated like this?

Was she always going to be forbidden to accept money or gifts? Then Heaven must send an angel to run the household. She couldn't. She sensed that Hannah was casting furtive glances at her as she moved about. Suddenly she planted herself squarely in front of Kate.

"Mrs. Luther."

Kate started. She had never thought that Hannah could talk so softly.

"You are crying," Hannah said, putting her hand on Kate's arm. "Come now, be like yourself again. You are always so cheerful."

Kate touched her fingers to her eyes. "Oh, Hannah," she half sobbed, "I must be very selfish. But I don't see how else . . ."

"Ach!" Hannah patted her arm, "that was just a little storm. Tomorrow the sun will shine much brighter."

Would it, Kate thought, still a bit resentfully. She didn't see how it could when everything had to be given away to beggars or was not even accepted like this gift from Salzburg. The more she thought about it the more disheartened she felt. Why had her Doctor been so positively stern about it?

She went about the afternoon's work without enthusiasm, not even caring to figure out how many to prepare supper for: several students, several translators, Cordatus, Jerome Weller, and a newcomer or so.

"Oh," she called to Hannah, "we'll prepare for the usual number. There's cheese and cold sausage and radishes and honey. Also, there's enough beer if I serve it carefully. The students can drink milk or water."

Luther surprised her by coming in early with young Jerome Weller on his arm. "Kate," he said, "you met Jerome this morning. Do you know that he intends to stay with us till he earns his degree?"

Kate expressed her pleasure at boarding such a promising young man and hoped that he would have no trouble in finding children to tutor. Then while the others were slowly straggling in and standing around talking, Luther quickly drew Kate aside.

"I made you feel bad," he said, patting her hand, "but I had to do it, Kate. I was so relieved I could give that money back to the Bishop of Salzburg."

"Why?"

"Because I'm sure it was meant as a bribe—to silence me."

Kate's eyes widened. Suddenly she saw the light. "And I acted like a foolish child," she murmured regretfully.

He gave her hand a warm squeeze. "Forget about it now and be happy again. Come, Kate," with a nod at the group waiting around the table, "let us have our supper."

He seemed in high spirits, she thought. After the prayer, when all were seated, he looked around with a curious smile. "Well," he queried, "what goes on in the world?"

No one answered immediately. Then a traveling scholar, whose name Kate had forgotten, took it upon himself to reply, "Much exploring, good Doctor, goes on in the New World of Columbus. The Spaniards especially are after the gold. They have brought back, also, strange fruits and plants and copper-colored savages. Some say they are cannibals. Others claim there is an ancient civilized kingdom there."

Luther nodded and looked thoughtful, "I hear the English and the French do much exploring, too. Only we Germans sit home poring over our books."

"If there are savages there," Jerome Weller ventured, "then surely there is need for us to send preachers."

"Most assuredly," Luther agreed. "Those poor people live in sin and darkness."

Kate spoke up quickly, "But they would kill the preachers!"

"Don't we kill, burn, hang, quarter, and torture people, too?" Luther replied. "All the greater is our shame, for we have the Word of God in its purity. But God knows what chaos our churches are in. The people and the preachers, too, are so ignorant that it wrings one's heart."

The scholar nodded gravely. "There is great spiritual darkness everywhere. And there is much oppression, superstition, and cruelty."

"To that I can testify!" Conrad Cordatus struck the table with his fist so forcibly that all looked up startled. "There is devilish cruelty," he said. "Did they not hold me imprisoned in a dank, dark dungeon with snakes for thirty-eight weeks? It is only due to God's great mercy that I am here."

There was more talk of current events. There was University small talk. After the singing of "The day is past and gone" and a prayer by Luther, the group adjourned.

In this way the summer passed. Gradually as the days grew shorter and the nights longer, Kate found more and more work awaiting her. She rose at five to help Hannah with breakfast and chores. Already there were several chickens cackling in the yard. Wolf had rigged up a temporary shack for them. There was a goose which Kate was fattening for the Christmas dinner. She hoped soon to find a better place of shelter for her fowl.

She was altogether too busy to think of her own welfare. But one cool morning in October, Kate felt a chill. And when Hannah poured beer into the kettle for the beer soup which alternated with barley soup for breakfast, the odor nauseated her. Running out into the yard she leaned against the pear tree, straining and retching till tears came to her eyes. The nausea persisted. Suddenly she felt two arms around her and a familiar voice exclaimed anxiously, "Kate! are you ill?"

She held on to the pear tree, her face buried in her right arm. "No," she choked, "it's nothing."

"Nothing! It's something, Kate. What is it?"

She raised her damp face and looked at him mistily. "Oh, Doctor . . . it's . . . it's just natural. I am going . . . to have . . . a child."

"A child?"

She caught a light in his strong, dark eyes, such as she had never seen there before. It must have been an illumination from heaven. His eyes were wet. "Oh, my Kate. A child coming to us? A gift of God! What could be more wonderful?"

"Then you are happy?"

"Happy!" he repeated. "I am overwhelmed, Kate. I

cannot believe it—such a priceless gift from heaven should be ours!"

And when she nodded glowingly, he asked, "When will the child come?"

She took his arm and, drawing it around her waist, said softly, "The child will come in June."

"As God wills," he said. "That we must never forget, Kate. Are you ready now to go back to the house? The morning air is cool."

Chapter 7

The garden had been plowed for the coming spring. The wilderness had been transformed into farm land. Luther himself had put in an order for seeds of all kinds from Erfurt. Fall was a good time for that. The chickens were laying eggs sparingly now, but in the spring Kate would set a number of hens for brooding. The goose was waddling around lonesomely and getting fatter every day. Next year there would be at least two geese—and also several ducks. A pair of pigeons had been offered Kate for next spring. A pig grunted contentedly in the makeshift pen. There would have to be more pigs—at least half a dozen—before too long. Her Doctor liked pork, roasted or fried or cooked—with sauerkraut. Kate would see to it that there would always be enough of what he liked. Then, too, she would sell the surplus and add to her income. She had already spoken to the Elector about a cow. He had promised to find one for her in the near future. Later on, there would be a horse, and a wagon as well.

Even a dog was there now. Wolf had brought the poor,

unhappy, shivering, black mongrel pup home one wet, fall evening. He had named him *Toelpel* because he was such an awkward clown. Now Hannah had threatened to bring a cat, because no household could be complete without a *Mietzi.*

Kate had also much sewing to do for the expected newcomer. Several times in the afternoon she had taken her sewing up to Doctor's study where the men were busy translating, and had sat there listening to them.

She loved these quiet afternoons. Usually she would slip out at four to help get supper ready. By five the translators, the students, the transients, the guests, and whoever belonged to the family would swarm into the big dining-room to be fed. After the usual devotion, Doctor would preach a short sermon in the little chapel. This was mostly for the students, but everyone was welcome. Kate was glad this happened only about twice a week. She was generally too tired to go, for she was beginning to rise earlier and earlier. She laughed with the rest when Doctor teased her, saying, "My Morning Star has to have time to set, else she can't rise again at four."

He had lately fallen into the habit of calling her the "Morning Star of Wittenberg." She did not mind his jesting, for then she knew that he felt well. When he turned quiet and seemed depressed, she knew that something was wrong. That rushing in his ears, that dizziness, and that pain that he had recently complained of frightened her terribly. Even the letter she had had from Aunt Lena saying that she was leaving the convent and coming to live with them did not quite cheer Kate. She was happy, of course, that Aunt Lena was coming. And her Doctor was pleased too. Having been head nurse at Nimbschen, Aunt Lena would be welcomed in any household for her helpfulness. She would be a great comfort, Kate thought, when the baby came.

But this past night had been a restless one for Kate. Maybe it was the excitement of Aunt Lena's letter, or the nearness to Christmas and the many things she still wanted to do. But mostly, she knew, it was worry about her Doctor. He seemed very heavyhearted. She missed his usual playful humor. In the morning when he rose she heard him sigh. He sat down at the breakfast table and rose again without touching his barley soup. When he turned to go to the lecture-room, she intercepted, "Doctor, what is bothering you?"

He put his hand on her arm. His deep, dark eyes were like troubled waters. "Pain," he said, "I am in pain. I think it's a stone. But worse than that is my spiritual pain. Oh, Kate, my soul is in great anguish!"

She stroked his arm, deeply sympathetic. "Any special reason?"

He leaned heavily against the door. "It seems they work together," he said, "the body and the soul. For when I feel better in body, I can much better fight these Sacramentarians who are such a great grief to me."

"Why can't you agree?" Kate asked. "Would that be so terrible?"

"You know my stand, Kate. God's word is supreme, understand it or not. But the Sacramentarians turn and twist a word around to agree with their reasoning. To this I will never give in."

Kate couldn't help seeing the anguish he was enduring. She took his hand and patted it. "I hope you'll be able to convince them," she said weakly.

"That isn't all," he breathed heavily, "that humanist, Erasmus, hounds me with his diatribes. He thinks I have been too severe in my writings. He is blind to the highest truth of salvation. He would like to be on my side, yet he is afraid to express himself. Then there is that English scoundrel King Henry VIII. Because he can't turn Protestant in name and induce me to sanction his divorce from Queen Catherine, he has written me a coarse, hateful letter."

Kate was at a loss what to say or do. "Are you writing a reply to Erasmus?" she asked.

"No! No! Heaven forbid! Oh, Kate, I am weary and weak. I'm attacked on all sides as if I were a wild beast. And yet all I have ever wanted to do is 'fight the good fight of faith'—preach to the people true salvation as God gave me to see it."

Kate nodded understandingly. "And that you have done, dear Doctor. But," she added earnestly, "I do think you should write Erasmus a letter in reply, else he will believe you are craven-hearted."

He looked uncertain. Then he answered slowly, "I think you are right, Kate. I will write him, but not just yet."

"And King Henry—can he really be so bad?"

He tore away from her. "Kate!" he said, so severely

that she shrank back at the intonation of his voice, "Henry is a bad man. He uses religion to cloak his lustful desire for women and his evil deeds."

Then he turned to go. When she saw him again at the supper table, there was still gloom in his eyes. He tried to be cheerful but conversation lagged. During the night Kate had an inspiration. A splendid idea, she thought jubilantly, and it will work. It will get him out of his melancholy mood.

When morning dawned her Doctor barely tasted food. Instead of going up to his study for translating, as he usually did, he told Kate he was going to drive out into the country with one of the professors. He did not know when he would return. Kate decided to carry out her plan.

When he was gone, she began to ransack the wardrobe for black clothes. She found a black bonnet and heavy veiling. She laid the things, together with her own black dress and a black mantle, out on her bed. When she had finished the afternoon chores, she retired to her bedroom, giving instructions to Hannah not to be disturbed. Then she proceeded to dress in the black outfit, with black shoes, and black stockings, a pair of black gloves, and a black veil. There was not a thread of white to be seen on her.

She picked up her black hymnbook and stationed herself near the door of the bedroom. Sitting there, hands demurely folded in her lap, holding the booklet, she waited. It could not be long before he would come now, she hoped. Suppertime was approaching. At last she heard horses' hoofs and wagon wheels in the yard. Again she waited. She heard him come up into the living-room.

She imagined how surprised he must be not to find her there. Then—he was coming toward the bedroom. Slowly he came closer. When he saw her he stopped short and stared. Finally he recognized her.

"Kate! what is this?"

She kept her head lowered and wiped her eyes with the bit of black lace.

"Kate! what are you up to?"

Then she rose, lifted the veil, dabbed at her eyes with the tiny handkerchief, gazed sadly into his face, and faltered, "Oh, Doctor, it is terrible! God . . . is . . . dead!"

Silence.

Then, like the sudden roar of a great waterfall, he burst into laughter.

"Kate!" and his voice had the merry old ring, "you are a deceiver. No! God is alive. And I thank God for you, my Kate. You have broken the evil spell."

After this Kate breathed freely once again. Now she could plan a happy Christmas celebration with Aunt Lena as one of the family. The old fat gander honking in the barnyard would soon be turned into roast goose.

Before Christmas Eve, however, the weather turned bad. Snow and ice made the already poor transportation much worse, so that Aunt Lena could not get to Wittenberg. Later, a letter came by messenger stating that she would take the first opportunity to come.

Kate went to St. Mary's to hear her Doctor preach. He came home on New Year's Day with a brand-new cloth coat lined with lambskin which the congregation had given him. Last year, he jestingly told her, they had rewarded him with a piece of fish—not a whole one but half a salmon.

"Well," Kate suggested, "this year's generosity might be followed by a fur coat next year."

The winter months finally gave way to spring. Aunt Lena, a quiet, motherly woman, moved in with them permanently. Kate had given her one of the rooms on the main floor. She had furnished it as well as she could and Aunt Lena did the rest. She immediately proved her worth by helping with the garden. Kate was feverishly anxious to get the garden seeded and the flowers planted. The barnyard population, which was very prolific, needed better housing. Wolf could not or would not do much since his hobby was to watch the birds and secretly to snare them. The women were more than ever busy with the house, so a man was found to take care of the outside work. He was to work for a small sum and board. Wolf, being neither servant nor boarder, neither paid nor received pay. He was just Wolf. He did mainly what it pleased him to do.

Kate was satisfied that things were going according to her wishes by the time June came around. She could see that her Doctor was worried as the time of her confinement neared. She surprised him profoundly one morning when he returned from lecturing by calling him into the bedroom. Aunt Lena placed a warm, squirming bundle in his arms. His first-born son! He held the infant gingerly, looked from him to his mother, raised his eyes to heaven and said, "God be praised for this precious gift of a son, and for the mother's safe delivery as well."

What will Elsie say to that?" Then, suddenly she felt ashamed. "Well, maybe it is just funny—Master Kate—and I ought to be glad he's feeling well enough to joke."

She sighed and decided to forget her annoyance. What a joy to see Elsie again after three years! And to show her that precious baby, little Hans! As she went on from task to task, and thought of all the happenings of the past few years, she almost forgot the present. It was not until she came into the living-room and placed a huge, wooden bowl of fruit in the center of the table that she heard horses' hoofs and the scraping of wheels.

"There she is," she called to Aunt Lena, running out.

The horses had come to a standstill. The driver jumped down and helped the comely young woman dismount. When Kate caught her first glimpse of Elsie's fair face, blond hair, and the becoming red cloth coat she wore over a dress of the same color, she rushed towards her.

"Oh, Elsie," she exclaimed, greeting her with a kiss, "you're prettier than ever!"

Elsie took Kate's arm and squeezed it affectionately. "You look good too, Kate. This life must agree with you."

Kate nodded. "Yes, but it means much work."

"Do you remember, Kate, what you said when Leonard Koppe brought us here?"

"The—sisters said that Wittenberg was ugly and the cloister—"

"Yes," Elsie interrupted animatedly, "and you said you could make something of this old Black Cloister."

"I'm trying to," Kate laughed, remembering. "I've got many plans for improving the rooms inside and many plans for beautifying the grounds. And also for gardens —flowers, vegetables, fruit trees. And hops for beer. But . . ." she sighed and hesitated, "all that takes more money than I have."

At the door they were met by Aunt Lena, carrying little Hans. When Elsie kissed him on his rosy cheek he crowed and laughed. "Oh, I love that baby, Kate. I almost envy you."

"You needn't," Kate said dryly. "If you'd marry, you'd have a baby and a home, too."

The old look of distress on Elsie's face made Kate laugh good-naturedly. "What! still so man-shy?" She shook her head as Elsie colored deeply and tried to hide it by caressing little Hans.

Aunt Lena said gently, "No, Kate, we can't all marry and have husbands and children. There are other things to do. At least Elsie feels that way . . ."

She paused at the sound of footsteps. "There is Doctor already," Kate exclaimed. "So early. Dinner isn't ready yet."

Luther came over to Elsie, hands extended. "My dear Elsie," he said cordially, "welcome in our cloister home."

"Oh, it's very homey and nice—especially that wonderful tile stove over there."

"Yes, that is a work of art," Luther agreed. "See, it has the pictures of the Evangelists." He pointed out other things to her, while Kate went to help Hannah with dinner and Aunt Lena took care of Hans. Elsie was still conversing with the Doctor when students and others began to straggle in and group around the table.

"Does Kate keep boarders?" she asked innocently.

"Yes," he laughed. "My Morning Star always has a houseful. Some are student boarders, three are refugees, another is an orphan, and several are transients. They travel, you see, and naturally make a stop off at Luther's Black Cloister."

Elsie looked up surprised. "They do?"

"Yes," he nodded, "some even come here to convalesce. I've found out myself that Kate is a good nurse and doctor."

"I know," Elsie agreed enthusiastically, "Kate is a remarkable nurse and she's a wonderful woman, too."

Luther folded his hands and all the others followed, bowing their heads in prayer. Then all were seated. The dinner was cheery. Elsie actually laughed at some of the witticisms of the learned Doctor.

"What's the news, you prelates?" he inquired jovially, looking along the table.

The shy students exchanged embarrassed looks. None spoke.

"Philip, what goes on everywhere? Surely our incomparable Greek scholar should know."

Melanchthon, who was almost a daily dinner guest, put down his bit of bread and wiped his mouth. Then, looking up, he said quietly, "The pea soup is excellent!"

Laughter from the students followed this sage remark. Kate colored but looked pleased. She picked up a bowl and, passing it on, said, "I hope you all like my pea puree and the sausage too. I had ordered herring . . ." her voice suddenly rose to a sharp shrill, "but I think the sea must have dried up because the fish didn't come."

There was general chuckling. One of the students rose and asked, "What would you do, Mrs. Luther, if the sea did actually dry up?"

Kate replied, "I'd buy a fish pond." Then she called to Hannah to bring on the sweet bread, the fruit and the nuts, whereupon the talk went on to other things.

The week was too short to show Elsie everything, to visit the Reichenbachs, Cranachs, and Melanchthons, and to talk over the old days at Nimbschen. Doctor, also, was anxious to persuade Elsie to come to Wittenberg and teach in a girls' school which he was going to organize. But Elsie was happy where she was. She hoped, however, to visit the Luthers again. With this promise, smiling, she departed.

Chapter 8

The months after Elsie's visit were passing quickly. Kate had stored away and salted, dried, or pickled vegetables and fruits for the winter. Her Doctor had helped her with a new well and with planning another garden. Now, on her advice and the physician's, he had also ordered tools for wood turning. The exercise was necessary for his bodily well-being.

Although little Hans was by now almost a year old, his father still went into ecstasies over the child. When Hans smiled for the first time, he was transported with delight. When Hans began to creep, he mentioned the fact in his letters. When he was about to take his first steps, Philip Melanchthon was called in to witness the performance.

Once Kate put him on his father's lap while she went to fetch the shoe he had lost. Little Hans sat there, suspiciously quiet, his face getting redder and redder. Even then the Doctor could not hide his admiration for his son's feat. "Kate," he exclaimed jocularly, "this little idiot has made a stink. Ah," he added, sobering, "how many a stink must not our heavenly Father bear from us mortals."

Kate asked him on one occasion, when Hans's crying disturbed their sleep, whether he wished himself back in single life.

"No," he assured her, "I still believe in marriage, in spite of all its discomforts and troubles."

He also expressed deep joy when she confided to him one day in April that there was another child coming in December.

"Then by all means," he urged, "let us have my parents visit us before it becomes too burdensome for you."

The old couple had intended to wait until summer, but now consented to come in May. As in the previous year, Kate and Hannah worked to get the housecleaning out of the way. A room adjoining Aunt Lena's was put in readiness for them. Hannah watched Kate's energy with amazement.

"You seem so happy," she remarked, the morning the parents were expected. "How can anyone be so happy?"

"I have much to be thankful for, Hannah. The most wonderful man in the world is my husband. And I'm thankful that he's well right now. And I have a precious little son, a dear old aunt, a comfortable home, and now the Doctor's parents are coming."

"To stay?"

"I hope so. If I can persuade them."

"But they will be much trouble and work!"

"Oh," Kate cut her short, "work is good for us. Why, Hannah, you're happy yourself."

"Yes, I am. I have a good mistress and master. And

I like to work in this place. When the air gets warm and the grass comes out green and the lilacs smell sweet—m'm!" She drew a deep breath.

"And don't forget the Elbe. The way it rolls along and hums its spring song is beautiful. Listen, Hannah," she called, starting down the circular stairs, "I hear Doctor's voice. They're here—Father and Mother are here. I wonder whether Peter brought them."

Aunt Lena heard her call and hurried after her with the baby. Her Doctor was leading them in. No, Peter was not there.

"Dear Father and Mother," Kate greeted them as she kissed them, "welcome a thousand times. See, here is my Aunt Lena with our darling little Hans. Isn't he sweet?"

It was plain that they were not accustomed to such outbursts of emotion. Old Hans Luther shook her hand heartily. A hint of a smile momentarily brightened old Margaret's face. The austere expression habitual to both of them gave way to a softer one. Kate thought that perhaps they had not expected such a warm welcome. She put her arm around the mother's spare, shrunken frame and, gazing into the wrinkled, weather-beaten old face, said lovingly, "Come, Mother, let us go to your bedroom so you can rest. You must be tired. Afterward you shall hold little Hans and then we will show you the garden."

She led them to the cozy little room she had furnished for them and helped the mother remove her cloth cloak. Meanwhile, Doctor Luther took off his father's heavy boots and helped him into his house slippers. Then they pulled up chairs in the living-room and, while Kate skipped down to see how Hannah was progressing with the dinner, Luther stayed to chat with his parents. They explained that they had driven with a good friend. Peter would visit them later. Soon Kate and Hannah came up with steaming platters of Kate's chicken and wild boar sent for the occasion by the Elector. There was hot boiled cabbage and carrots, chunks of good fresh bread, and a great sweet dumpling with fruit for dessert. The town council had sent wine in honor of the parents' visit.

Kate placed the father and the mother next to their son at the table. They stood modestly aside while the students, guests, refugees, and all the usual company streamed in to dinner. She thought at first they looked a bit bewildered. But after a short prayer in which Luther asked the blessing and thanked God for the privilege of serving his parents in his own home, all were seated and the meal progressed in the accustomed way.

Father Hans seemed to take a lively interest in the conversation, Kate thought. Several times she thought she detected a sparkle of fun in his eyes that reminded her of the twinkle in her Doctor's eyes when he was in a merry mood. The mother's impassive face, however, remained resigned. She seemed quietly happy. But Kate could easily imagine what stern disciplinarians both of them had been to young Martin. Yet it was because they meant to implant honesty and obedience to God and his elders in his heart. They knew of no other way.

Seeing that young Hans was squirming in Aunt Lena's lap, Kate took him from her and held him up for his father to see. The baby laughed and squealed happily.

"You naughty, young rascal," Luther joked, "why do we all love you so and watch every little tooth that shows?"

"Looks like a husky fellow," someone remarked.

"He'll be like his grandfather," another called, whereupon all smiled, old Hans looked pleased and young Hans squealed.

"Well," remarked Luther, "this afternoon my Sanhedrin has another tussle with Job. Father," he said, looking at the elder man, "you have no idea how Job resists us at every turn. The Hebrew will not be made a German."

After grace the students and others dispersed. Luther lingered a while with Kate and his parents before joining the translators. Kate helped clear the table, saw Aunt Lena put little Hans to bed for his afternoon nap, and directed Hannah to do the rest, while she went out with her husband and his parents to look at the garden. First, they had to look at the bench which their son and Wolf had made under the old pear tree.

"Is this the pear tree where Staupitz comforted you?" old Hans wanted to know.

"Yes, Father. It was under this tree where I suffered such severe mental anguish and knew not where to turn for help. I was tormenting myself by a system of penance —pain, punishment, expiation—and was sick and despairing. Then Brother Staupitz counseled me not to look to my own acts by which I could never satisfy God. 'No,' he said, 'rather look to Christ, your loving Saviour, who suffered for you and earned your redemption. Hang on to Him and God cannot turn you down.' "

The old folks listened with pious, bowed heads. Mother Margaret's eyes dimmed with tears. "A good man," she murmured, "thank God for good Brother Staupitz. God rest his soul."

A cool wind came from the river. Kate took off her shawl and threw it around the mother's shoulders. "The spring air has a sharp sting," she said, "but if you're not too tired, Mother, I'd like you to see Wolf's little turner shop, where Doctor sometimes works with him. They make toys for Hans and chairs and benches and tables."

The shop door was ajar and as they peeped in, Kate exclaimed, "Here is Wolf at work now. Look, Doctor, what he's doing."

Luther laughed. "A hobbyhorse, is it not? Show it to my father and mother." Wolf held up the half-finished object and nodded shyly. "Little Hans must have something to ride on, else he'll never be a man."

Old Hans chuckled and nudged his son. "I think they're spoiling him."

Old Margaret looked serious. "Don't bring him up too soft," she said. "Life is hard."

They wandered on and Kate pointed out her vegetable garden, her flower garden, the little corner for herbs and the new fruit trees. Yes, Mother must also see the hens, the ducks, and the geese.

"We will have some eggs for supper," Kate promised. "And look here," she laughed, opening the door of a small pen, "pigs! You know, your son likes pork roast."

Even old Margaret smiled when the two pigs looked up from under their overhanging ears and grunted.

"Now," said old Hans, "you must get a cow, a horse or two, a few sheep, some goats, and . . ."

"Oh, we shall," Kate interrupted breathlessly. "The Elector has already promised us a cow for fall."

Luther patted her shoulder good-naturedly. "Yes, my Master Kate has great plans and ideas. And I never interfere, for she is a master manager. She can make something out of nothing." He put his arm around her shoulder and drew her close, while they stood gazing out over the Elbe.

"It looks to me," commented old Hans, "as if you two were very happy."

"We are happy," the Doctor admitted. "I love my Kate—my Morning Star—Father. And since I've been married to her, I think often of what good Mrs. Cotta used to say to me, 'there is nothing lovelier on earth than a woman's love, if you can get it.' " He turned quickly. "But I must get back to Job now."

While he hurried on, Kate followed more slowly with the old folks. As she looked at the two shriveled old bodies, with their nut-brown faces, a surge of love overwhelmed her. "Father and Mother," she said, "could you not stay here and live with us the remaining years of your life?"

They looked at her and at each other and shook their heads solemnly. "No, child," Mother Margaret said, "we are poor peasants, not fit to live the life you live."

Old Hans threw back his shoulders. "No, Mother," he contradicted, "we are no longer poor. That was in the beginning. Now," he added proudly, "I have even enough to leave something to my children."

The mother nodded silently. Kate looked at both, surprised.

"But," she urged, "we would love to have you. You know, I never had any parents at all. And it would be nice for little Hans." She caught Mother Margaret's hand. "You could live undisturbed in that little room."

But no! They would not hear of it. They would come again for a visit, God willing. Next time they would bring Peter. There were nieces and nephews that wanted to come. It was with real heartache that Kate bade them farewell after their two weeks' visit. When they had left she realized that perhaps they were right in preferring to live by themselves. So much work—this spring planting. So many visitors and guests at the table every day. People seemed to come from everywhere. All the homeless, the needy, the shelterless, the exiled, the refugees, the sorrowing that sought to find comfort or shelter or food here—not to speak of the princes, electors, scholars, and other famous individuals! They came from England, Denmark, Austria, Holland, France, Poland, Italy, Bohemia, Moravia, and everywhere.

No wonder Kate was expanding her hennery and looking for more garden land. She needed a garden for the hops and barley from which to brew the beer that was consumed by all these people. What else were they to drink? Milk? There would never be enough in all this world, Kate thought, for everyone to drink milk. Besides, you had to save out enough for butter and cheese. The demand for cheese was unending. Kate possessed a number of good recipes for manufacturing the various kinds.

As for drinking water, good water was scarce. Some people never drank it. Some brought water from the Elbe, then boiled and cooled it. A few hauled water from a well miles away.

So far Kate was content to use whatever water she could get. Now, since Aunt Lena had taught her how to use the old beerhouse, she could make almost enough to quench the thirst of the many guests at mealtime.

Chapter 9

Kate's pregnancy did not worry her as much as it did her Doctor. She could see that he was suffering, and she feared a repetition of the spell in winter. She had thought to cheer him with the promise of another child—perhaps another son. A bit timidly she had asked, "Doctor, if this child should be a girl will you be just as happy?"

"Certainly, Kate. Certainly."

"Then I wish for a girl."

"God grant she be well and you keep well, dear Kate. Let us not forget to pray at all times."

Again he seemed to rally and went about joking, lecturing, preaching, translating, writing letters, receiving important visitors, and sparing himself at no time. Still Kate kept anxious eyes on him.

"Why don't you go to that breakfast Hans Loeser invited you to?" she asked one morning, a little later. "It would do you good."

He turned away. "I care not to eat or drink or see anyone."

"But, Doctor, it will be like medicine for you to get out. Please go!"

He finally went. Later he came back with Jonas. When Kate saw them walk in the garden, she felt relieved that she had invited Jonas and his wife for the evening. But before they arrived she suddenly heard her husband cry, "Kate! Kate! Come here! I need you."

She ran to comfort him.

"Oh," he moaned, "my head is bursting! It's like the sea. The whole ocean seems to be roaring through my ears and in my head. Oh, the pain in my head! Kate, help me to bed."

She steadied him, but at the bedroom door he sank down in a dead faint. Kate motioned to Jonas and his wife who had just come in to help her get him into bed. They revived him with cold water. She heard him murmur, "Oh, God, my God, I thank Thee for having brought me to the knowledge of Thy dear Son, my Saviour. This I have taught according to Thy holy Word. Oh, Lord, God, if it be Thy will to take me hence—"

His words became inaudible. Another swoon seized him. Kate felt his pulse. His body was getting cold. Tears were streaming down her face as the physician, Augustine Schurf, entered.

"Hot water vessels," he ordered, "and heat the covers."

Kate hurried out. At the same time she dispatched Wolf for Bugenhagen. Then she watched anxiously while Schurf smothered the patient with heat. Gradually he revived. Smiling wanly he asked, "Where is my darling little Hans?"

Kate brought him in on her arm, cooing, smiling, and waving his chubby hands. His father watched him, then said, "My dearest Kate, God will take care of both of you. I pray you to submit to His gracious will. Keep to the Word of God. Always, dear Kate. And remember that you are my honorably wedded wife." He pointed to several silver cups. "That is all I can leave you, Kate."

Kate swallowed hard. "Oh, my dearest Doctor," she managed to say, "if it is God's will, then I would rather have you with Him than stay with me. But so many good Christians need you still. I commend you to God's care."

He fell back exhausted. The hot cloths and applications were bringing on profuse perspiration. When he closed his eyes, relaxed, and fell asleep, all stole quietly out of the room except Bugenhagen who had come to pray with him.

Schurf gave Kate further instructions and left with the Jonases. Every now and then she peeped into the room where Bugenhagen kept watch. Seeing that the patient was still asleep, she thanked God and went to tell Aunt Lena and faithful Hannah and Wolf that he was not getting worse. She advised them to go to bed. About midnight, when the patient was still deeply asleep, she suggested to Bugenhagen that he go home.

Morning dawned at last. Kate was overjoyed to see her Doctor get up. He did not refuse the barley broth she offered him. He was far from strong. As the days went on, he still complained of feeling weak. "And the spiritual anguish," he said. "It comes back again and again. Oh, Kate, the agonies of death and damnation! Our dear Saviour suffered them, too. Oh, pray, pray every minute!"

He resumed his place at the family table and, though he was weak, tried to be his own cheery self with the boarders and guests. For a while everything looked brighter although rumors of the plague near Wittenberg dampened everyone's spirits.

Then, one day, Bugenhagen came over looking solemn. "It's here," he said, "the plague is in Wittenberg now."

"Where?" Kate asked, terror-stricken.

"It began in Fisher's suburb and seems to be moving right up here. Already people are leaving the city."

"Oh, good God!" escaped Kate, "then we have to move, too, Doctor. Don't we?"

"Kate," he put his arm around her shoulder, drew her close, and looked lovingly into her eyes. "My dearest Kate, where is your faith? It's not like you to run away."

She trembled and let her head rest heavily against him and dabbed at the tears that insisted on making their way down her cheeks. "But I'm afraid—afraid for little Hans—and afraid for you—and myself," she faltered, "and that new little life that is within me."

Bugenhagen tried to comfort her. "Kate," he said, patting her arm in a fatherly way, "you surprise me. Usually you are so strong and steady you are an example to us men. Now don't be so broken up about it. God lives. He knows all, sees all, and will take care of us all."

"Then you think we . . . have . . . to stay?"

Both men nodded. "Definitely. We cannot leave our post of duty," Luther said, "and run the minute danger threatens."

"Come what will," Bugenhagen added, "we must stay

here with our congregation to comfort the sick and dying."

Kate inwardly shuddered. "Those sick and dying of this awful plague," she thought despairingly.

No wonder students and professors were fleeing. Bugenhagen said that the University was to be removed to Jena. The city was panic-stricken. Even the Elector was not above fear. He sent word to Luther to move like the rest and save his life.

But Luther refused, as Kate knew he would. "Our fervent prayers," he told her, "will save us. In fact," he added, "I think the fear is as bad as the pest itself. If you are still so afraid, Kate . . ."

"No! No!" Kate suddenly experienced an influx of strength. She felt able to steel herself against the inevitable. Her Doctor, as usual, was right. It would be unworthy to run away. Besides, what good was faith if it wilted like a broken flower? No, faith should be strong, like the trunk of an oak, strong enough to lean on in a time of trouble.

She could see how relieved her Doctor was at this complete change in her. Aunt Lena seemed to breathe easier and even Hannah felt less afraid. "Mistress," she said one morning, "if you in your pregnant condition can stay and the Doctor with his poor health, then, surely I can stay too. But you know," she went on ominously, "the city is almost empty. The market place is deserted. Farmers don't dare come into town. Soon we'll have nothing to eat."

"No, Hannah," Kate resolutely countered, "don't worry. God won't let us starve. There'll always be something."

Kate's faith was put to severe tests during the anxious weeks that followed. When the first long procession of mourners passed the house to bury their dead in graves that were in the rear of the cloister, she couldn't suppress a feeling of revulsion. When the burials became a daily occurrence and she already had counted eighteen, she became less horrified. Day after day, when she saw her Doctor start out for the underground chambers to which many of the luckless victims had been removed by their kin, she felt more pity than fear. She watched him leave the house, head erect, to comfort each poor, stricken soul. He read psalms, spoke tenderly to them of the joy in heaven, prayed, and administered the holy Sacrament to the dying. His very presence in those dark chambers of death, Kate thought, must have given those sufferers a foretaste of heaven. When he returned, weary from these daily missions, Kate knew that his decision to stay had been right. Who else would have prayed with the burgomaster's wife? Kate actually cried when Luther came home and said sadly, "Well, Tilo's wife is in heaven now, too."

"Oh, Doctor, does he know? Poor Tilo!"

"Yes, he came in just as I was praying with her and holding her in my arms to give her relief."

Kate couldn't suppress the tears then. "Poor Tilo and his little children. Oh, Doctor," with a sudden impulse she threw her arms around him, "I am so glad you were with her and could help ease her last breath! You are such a comfort—such a rock of faith."

Her head was on his shoulder. She was still crying

softly. His own eyes brimmed over as he patted her arm and observed, half jestingly, "A rock of faith! Why, my darling Kate, look! I'm crying like a woman—like yourself."

He held her close for a moment, then released her. "Kate," he said, deeply moved, "I can never thank the good God enough for you. A friendly, godly wife like you is God's greatest gift to a man."

She bowed her head modestly, "I have prayed to do His will as you taught me to." She smiled gratefully then, thinking how impossible it would have seemed a month ago to smile with so many sick and dying about her. But she wept soon again when Jonas came over with the news that they had lost their small son, and when Bugenhagen came to tell them that Roerer's pregnant wife had died in the parsonage. So frightened had Bugenhagen's wife, Walburga, now become that Kate asked George Roerer and Bugenhagen to leave the pest-infested parsonage and move in with them.

Kate made this request in spite of the fact that she was in the same condition in which Mrs. Roerer had been. Two of Luther's nieces who had come several weeks before were down with light cases. Physician Schurf had brought his wife here for them to take care of. It seemed to Kate that Hannah Schurf was getting worse, so ill and weak she was.

And when, one day, Madeline von Mochau, a family friend, was prostrated by fever and weakness, Kate knew that the dreadful scourge had entered the house. But her faith was firm, her head clear, and her hand steady. Faithfully she cared for Madeline and Hannah Schurf, who were soon covered with boils. When the physician came to lance the boils, Kate helped to press out the poison and daily dressed the wounds. Soon Madeline became so deathly ill that Kate remarked to her husband, "If she lives through this, it will be a miracle of God."

"There will be more miracles, Kate, than we have eyes to see."

"But Hannah doesn't improve one bit. She's just weak and ill."

"Give her time," he said. "What I have seen of this is enough to drag down a strong man. And," he advised, "let Aunt Lena help you. She is a good nurse.'

Madeline recovered, but Hannah could not gain strength and still needed nursing. Then little Hans, who had been whimpering for days, became very ill.

"Is it the scourge?" Luther asked his wife, turning pale as a sheet.

"I think not," she comforted him. "Aunt Lena and I think it's just a bad case of teething. He hasn't eaten for three days."

She heard his sigh of relief and, although his spiritual suffering was by no means over, he attempted to make light of the whole tragic situation by jesting about their hospital and calling himself "Brother Cure-all Salubris" and "Brother Hospitaler."

Only when he learned that a faithful Bavarian minister of the cross had been publicly burned to death, did he break out into lamentation. "Oh, why would not God let me, too, die a martyr to His word? Why must I struggle on with my miserable life while they give theirs for the Saviour?"

Kate listened patiently to this outburst. Then she said, "Because God still needs you here on earth."

"Oh," he sighed, "God has many others to do His work. No one person is so important to Him that He can't do without him. Kate, would that all those who hate me so could see the misery of my heart! How they all rage against me because of my love for Christ! What could ever comfort me if the Saviour were to forsake me?"

Kate spoke words of cheer. "He will not forsake you," she said calmly. "He is only testing your faith."

And once again he rose above his suffering. "I will go on, Kate. He will be my strength. Keep on praying, dear heart. Pray for me. God can shorten these evil days."

Kate knew, by the deep glow in his eyes, by the turmoil that had been churning in his soul, that he was bursting with some great song or sermon. And when he left her to go to his study, her eyes followed him thoughtfully.

One morning early in October, he came to her with a paper in his hand. "Read this, Kate," he said, an unearthly look in his eyes as he handed her the paper. She read:

Ein' feste Burg ist unser Gott
A mighty fortress is our God.

Tears filled her eyes as she read on:

He helps us free from ev'ry need
That hath us now o'ertaken.

Looking up, she said, "You must have thought of all the pest-sick people in our house who are all getting better now—our little Hans and even Hannah Schurf."

He nodded silently and waited for her to finish.

> Though devils all the world should fill,

Again she interrupted herself, "Oh, Doctor, was it not like that when you went to Worms in 1521?"

Again he nodded, and she read on:

> Take they then our life,
> Goods, fame, child, and wife, . . .
> The Kingdom ours remaineth.

"Oh, Doctor," she said, handing it back to him, "this is inspired. It is a great song . . ."

"Enough!" he interrupted her, then stood up and began to pace the room. "Give the glory to God where it belongs. I was only the instrument. But . . ." he stopped short in front of her. "Now for the music. To set it to fitting music. I have a melody in my head . . ."

Kate merely nodded her approval.

"I need help," he went on impatiently, "professional help. I know enough music for ordinary purposes but it must be professionally done."

"Send it to Spalatin," Kate suggested readily. "He's at the Elector's court and in good grace there. Or perhaps the great musician Walther . . ."

"That's it, Kate," he broke in excitedly. "I'll send word at once."

He had not long to wait before John Walther, composer and organist, made his appearance at the house.

"I have come on the Elector's orders," he said, "to assist with putting this powerful song of yours to music. I intend to stay until the task is finished."

Overjoyed, Luther asked, "In spite of the pest?"

"They tell me it's over. Some students and professors have already come back."

"It's over in our house," Kate sighed, "with nothing worse than the two pigs we lost. I've been disinfecting every room."

Then, for the next three weeks she heard more music in her house than she had ever heard in her life. Her Doctor and John Walther were busy composing music for several hymns besides "A Mighty Fortress." Mathias Weller, another musician of note, joined them at times. While Luther was busy lecturing in the morning, Walther composed. In the afternoon the sound of singing and playing the lute came from the study. Every evening after the five o'clock supper and prayers, Luther started the ball rolling again by asking, "How about singing—trying out the new *Feste Burg?*"

When Luther picked up his lute and commenced to sing, all those present joined in. After singing one or two simpler hymns, they ended with rehearsing Luther's new "Battle Hymn."

Kate knew how much her Doctor was enjoying this for he loved music next to theology. "Whoever doesn't like music," he told them, "must be a stone or block. Music drives away sorrow and care. It is an antidote against temptation and evil thoughts."

"Especially music set to such words as *Ein Feste Burg,*" observed Walther. "Doctor Luther, it is a song that will be sung by generations to come."

"A song to inspire one with God-given courage," added Weller. "A powerful song."

Luther looked deeply thoughtful. "Truly," he said, "we have need of such a song to encourage us, and also to thank our God that this terrible plague has subsided."

When the hands of the clock neared nine, Kate remarked that it was time to retire.

"I think we all know the song by now," she said, "and the congregation will learn it from us."

"You heard," warned Luther. "So now to pray and sleep."

Chapter 10

With the return of the university professors and students, life in Wittenberg resumed its normal routine. Frosty fall nights destroyed every last pest germ, and soon the trying days of the summer were forgotten.

Kate was busier than ever. After the birth of Elizabeth early in December, her restless energy again drove her on relentlessly. She could depend on Aunt Lena to care for the baby, although the infant was not thriving as she wished, and to supervise little Hans's activity. Kate went about the numerous tasks that daily awaited her. With the ever-growing household, the ever-increasing number of visitors, student boarders, beggars, and borrowers, Kate was glad that her Doctor's salary had been increased a second time. He was still far too generous in giving away things. But Kate always managed some improvement.

Almost all the little rooms upstairs were in use by this time. This spring Kate again had the kitchen white-washed. She had the hearth enlarged and equipped with firedogs to hang the copper kettles on. She had added a huge three-legged iron pot that could be set on the fire directly and a revolving spit to roast young suckling pig or the chunks of wild boar meat or venison so frequently sent them by Elector John. Kate had added shovels, tongs, two-pronged forks, flesh hooks and other much needed tools. There was a reconditioned cupboard, scoured and scrubbed and made to look like new, in which the new tin, pewter, copper, and wooden dishes could be neatly packed away. Kate had also invested in some of the new stone pottery which she found so useful for storing milk, now that they had a cow. The new wooden churn was put to use every week to produce fresh butter. Wicker baskets of every size and description stood in handy places or hung from the ceiling. She had even hung up a picture displaying an assortment of fish. Now, as she looked about her kitchen, she felt proud and happy.

She had worked hard, too, with Hannah and Wolf to turn some vacant space into a fresh-smelling room to store vegetables and fruits for the winter. Another room had been converted into servants' quarters. There already was a barnyard boy, and Kate foresaw that there would be others before too long.

The thing she was happiest about was the bathroom which was still in the making. A wooden tub had been ordered from Nuremberg. On the wall already hung a precious mirror brought from Venice by one of Luther's admirers. She was waiting now for a stand she had ordered, and was scouting around for a suitable stone pitcher and washbowl. So enthusiastic was Kate about her plans for a bathroom that she freely discussed it with her friends. Margaret Reichenbach, Barbara Cranach, and Walburga

Bugenhagen spoke encouragingly. So did others. Only Katherine Melanchthon, who rarely visited Kate, had little to say. She neither approved nor disapproved. Kate complained of this to her Doctor one evening when they were sitting up late alone.

"I don't understand Katherine," she observed, "she's not like formerly, when I used to go there before I was married."

"She may have troubles of her own."

"I wouldn't know what, Doctor. Philip is a good husband and she has little Philip and her little girl."

"Well, Master Kate, I'd advise you to forget about it. Maybe some other time she'll seem different. Or, maybe you'll be different . . . yourself."

The way he said "Master Kate" and the way he emphasized "yourself" made Kate look up quickly. She was about to make some sharp reply when he laughed. "How about that fine, perfumed soap you made, Kate? Did you show that to Katherine, too?"

Kate nodded. "Of course I did. And she said she wished she could make some too. I gave her a piece, but I don't think she even wanted to accept it."

"And you need it badly enough for your own household. Really, Kate, how you manage to feed and shelter all these people and still make all these improvements is beyond me."

Kate jumped at a chance she had been waiting for. "I need to do much more, Doctor. In that small garden I can't raise enough vegetables to feed the people who come here."

She paused and he looked at her expectantly. "Yes?"

"I need more garden space and soon, you know, Peter will come to help us. Couldn't we buy a little plot somewhere?"

"Kate, we're in debt as it is."

"That's exactly why I want another garden. I'll get us out of debt. Think of all the feed I could raise. We need hay for the horse and cow and fresh green things for the pigs. All that I now have to buy."

"Do you want to sell or pawn the last three beautiful goblets?"

"Oh, Doctor," Kate was becoming exasperated, "can't you see how much cheaper it would be in the end to buy that land?"

He remained firm. "No, Kate, not now. Wait at least a year or two, Kate. Think of the expense we've just had with the kitchen and your bathroom."

Kate turned away disheartened. This time she could not persuade him, but she would—next time. Anyway, she reasoned, perhaps he was right. For one thing, baby Elizabeth was a great care. She didn't seem to improve. Even with Aunt Lena's help, taking care of the two children was a real task. Little Hans was inclined to be naughty.

Added to these cares was all this unrest, all this talk about "visitations." Every day, at every meal, the learned theologians discussed this topic. Every day brought new guests to the table—people who came from everywhere. There was much complaint of the ignorance of preachers and teachers. Not only were some of the preachers uninformed, she heard, but they actually used quotations from the Bible as "a cloak of maliciousness."

Melanchthon had been commissioned to prepare some "regulations and instructions" in this matter. Kate had learned from her Doctor that these articles comprised the fundamental principles of Evangelical doctrine as they were to be accepted by the congregations. They were drawn up especially for the common, unlettered folk who knew little or nothing about Christian faith and life.

Kate heard much of the dogmatic disputes that followed. What she didn't hear herself, her Doctor told her. He approved of Melanchthon's draft. So did the Elector who had it published. She was relieved to see her Doctor so undisturbed by all the talk and argument. Finally at one of their meetings the men decided on visitations on a large scale. Committees were appointed consisting of a theologian, several laymen, a lawyer, and a councilor of state. These were to visit the various parishes in electoral Saxony.

How glad Kate was to hear that her Doctor had been assigned districts not too far from Wittenberg! Since Bugenhagen had already left the city, Luther substituted in his congregation during his absence. Besides all his other work, he now preached three or four times a week. When he returned from one of his visitation trips, his report of the poverty and destitution, the ignorance of the common people, the drunkenness and immorality among the clergy was so vivid that Kate threw aside everything to listen.

"God help me," he sighed, "what misery I have seen! Kate, you have no idea how they live."

"Who? The priests or the people?"

"Both. We found in Torgau an old priest who could hardly repeat the Lord's Prayer and the Creed. But he was good at driving devils out of people. That was his main business."

"If anyone else but you told me this," Kate confessed, "I wouldn't believe it."

He shook his head sadly. "It's only too true. Most of the peasants didn't know the Lord's Prayer. Some knew not a single prayer. Others couldn't learn one because all the prayers were too long."

"How sad, Doctor."

"And as for schools, Kate, there aren't any in most places. No schools at all. How are children to be taught the Ten Commandments, the Lord's Prayer and the Creed, without which we cannot accept them for Communion?"

"What they need," Kate said simply, "is the catechism you have told me about."

He nodded solemnly. "I'll write one," he said. "A big catechism to instruct the clergy how to teach people. And a small one for children and for the common folks who have so little understanding. May God help them out of this spiritual darkness."

He went on many more short journeys. Always, before going, he would kiss Kate and Hans goodbye and inquire solicitously about baby Elizabeth. Always he returned so weary and exhausted that Kate worried about him as much as she did about the baby.

"No wonder," she told Aunt Lena, as they sat knitting one afternoon. "anyone would get tired riding in those clumsy wagons over those terrible roads that are nothing but cow paths."

"I know," Aunt Lena nodded, clicking her needles, "I had enough of it when I came here from Grimma. You feel every bump and every stone. And often there are deep ruts so that the wagon rocks to and fro, and it's dangerous."

Kate made a grimace of disgust. "It's not quite so bad when the weather is dry. Then you have only the dust to swallow. But if it rains, mud splashes all over you and you're likely to get stuck in a mudhole. And," letting her knitting drop, "no one does a thing about it. Not even the Elector."

Aunt Lena shook her head. "It's a dreadful waste of time, too," she observed. "Dr. Luther told me that five miles a day is considered good traveling."

Kate picked up her knitting, then held it poised a moment while she looked up to reply. "You know that last trip he made from Wittenberg to Gotha is forty miles. Do you know how long it took them?' She waited expectantly, then supplied the answer herself, "Eight days."

At that moment Wolf came in with Hans on his arm and Toelpel, the dog, slinking at his heels.

"It is beginning to rain," he announced, "and the spring air is sharp again. How about a fire?" he asked. "The baby needs warmth and the Doctor might come home cold, too."

Kate was glad when he did come the same evening and there was a warm room for him. She saw at a glance how much this visitation had taken out of him. Again he complained of the general ignorance among the people. He had mingled with them and talked with them and was more than ever distressed that boys and girls were growing up without schools. He had told the Elector's Chancellor Brueck about it. He had thought that Brueck was a good man who was trying to help the Reformation, but he had received an unsatisfactory response from Brueck.

Tired out as he was, he went to lecture, as usual, the next morning from seven to nine. After that he met the many visitors who daily besieged him. Kate saw him come from his study in deep conversation with a scholarly man she did not know. She guessed that he was bringing the scholar in for dinner. But the stranger went away. Inadvertently Kate found herself looking at another man who had suddenly appeared from nowhere. She could not understand why she was staring at the back of this man who was advancing toward her husband until a realization flashed through her mind that paralyzed her with fear. The man, not aware of her presence, was clutching a knife in his right hand behind his back.

Kate's heart stood still. He was going to harm her Doctor. She wanted to scream, to motion to her husband, but could not. Then a strange thing happened. Luther rapidly stepped up to the man and in his hearty way asked, "Well, my good man, what can I do for you?" The weapon clattered to the floor. The man sank to his knees. Haltingly he confessed that he had meant to kill Luther and now implored his forgiveness. Kate was still trembling when she saw her Doctor talk kindly to the man and lead him to the table. Now she knew what he had meant when he told her that there were people who would be glad to kill him.

Later, when she caught him alone for a moment, she whispered, "Doctor, I saw that man and I was sick with fright. Did you realize what his intentions were?"

He nodded. "I suspected it. But you see, God has a way of protecting His own."

"It must be so," she sighed, "for I thought you were lost." After a while she asked, "Are you preaching again tonight?"

"Yes, at the chapel. For the students mainly. And tomorrow for Bugenhagen at the Castle Church. Will my Kate be there?"

"No," she said, pointing to Aunt Lena, who was coming toward them with baby Elizabeth, "I am too worried about our baby."

Aunt Lena put the whimpering infant in her mother's arms, saying, "The child is restless and feverish."

Kate held her close and attempted to comfort her. "I don't know, Doctor, what is the trouble. When I asked Schurf, he shook his head and said she had a poor start in life because of the plague and everything."

"If we could just get her to feed normally," Aunt Lena observed, "but she doesn't seem to care for anything."

Luther stepped up to his wife and gazed at the infant with tender, anxious eyes. "My poor little one," he said, touching her silky, yellow hair, "she is so sweet. I pray God may let us keep her. Now," lingeringly, "I must leave."

The women's eyes followed his retreating figure, then looked at each other. Aunt Lena was first to speak.

"It always goes straight to my heart," she said, "how so great a man and so wonderful a scholar as Dr. Luther, can feel so deeply about a poor little baby."

"Oh, he feels for everyone," Kate replied. "He has suffered so much himself that he can't help feeling for others."

The chapel bell began ringing, and Hannah and Dorothy, a new servant, passed through the room on their way to the service.

"I wouldn't miss a single sermon of Dr. Luther if I could help it," Hannah called in passing.

"Neither would I," Dorothy chimed in.

Kate nodded absently. "I'd like to go myself, but the little one needs me."

Baby Elizabeth struggled through all of July. On the third day of August, her little heart beat its last. Both parents grieved deeply.

Soon, however, Kate realized that there would be another babe to fill her empty arms. Baby Madeline was born the following May. Luther was so overjoyed that he invited friends and sponsors to a baptismal dinner.

When the child was only four months old, he journeyed to Marburg, where he expected to stay for some time. Continued religious wranglings and discussions among the agitators required his presence. He wrote his wife a letter from there: "To Master Kate, my dearly beloved wife, greetings!" He described his living quarters, wrote in detail about the transactions, inquired about her health, told her about his own. He sent greetings to Aunt Lena and all the household and many kisses to little Hans and the baby. How glad he was, he added, that already little boys and girls here were being instructed and taught to pray.

He wrote the following letter to Hans:

"Grace and peace in Christ, my dear little son. I am glad to hear that you are studying and saying your prayers. Continue to do so, my son, and when I come home I will bring you a pretty present. I know a lovely, pleasant garden where many children are; they wear golden jackets, and gather fine apples and pears, and cherries, and purple plums and yellow plums under the trees, and sing and run and jump, and are happy, and have pretty little ponies with golden reins and silver saddles. I asked the man who owned the garden who they were. He said, 'They are the children who say their prayers and study, and are good.' Then I said, 'Dear man, I also have a son whose name is Hans Luther. May he come into the garden and eat the sweet apples and pears, and ride a fine pony and play with these children?' Then the man said, 'If he says his prayers and is good, he may come into the garden, and Phil and Justy, too, and when they all come, they shall have whistles and drums and fifes, and they shall dance, and shoot with little crossbows.' Then he showed me a fine, large lawn in the garden for dancing, where hung real golden whistles and fine silver crossbows. But it was yet early, and the children had not finished eating, and I could not wait to see them dance, so I said to the man, 'My dear sir, I must go and write at once to my dear little Hans about all this, so that he will say his prayers and study and be good, and so that he may come into the garden. And he has an Auntie Lena whom he must bring with him.' Then the man said, 'All right. Go and tell him about it.' So, dear little Hans, study and say your prayers, and tell Phil and Justy to say their prayers, too, so that you may all come into the garden together. God bless you. Give Aunt Lena my love and a kiss from me. Your loving father, MARTIN LUTHER."

In another letter he told of a panic brought on by a new pestilence, the English sweat. People were attacked by sudden fever, thirst, sweat, pain, great exhaustion, and then succumbed with fearful rapidity.

Kate was not surprised when her husband returned about the middle of October, much sooner than he had expected. The conference had come to a sudden close because of the dreaded sweat.

"It's here in Wittenberg, too," she told him ominously.

"It is deadly when it strikes," he agreed. "But, Kate, the fear of it is deadly, too. One night I, myself, awoke in a terrific sweat. Fever and fear tormented me. Had I given in, I would most certainly have been struck down. But I jumped out of bed, put on dry clothes, prayed, and went out into air."

Kate at first shook her head unbelievingly. But when, a few nights later, he routed Chancellor Brueck and a few other acquaintances out of their beds with brisk words, so that they afterward laughed at their fears, she became convinced that her Doctor was right.

Fortunately for all, the fear and sweat itself soon subsided. The members of Kate's household went about routine duties—the Doctor lecturing, translating, preaching, and Kate working outside and in the kitchen, superintending everything. She was especially happy the next few months to be able to devote herself to her husband and her two children. The new baby was not only healthy but displayed the most angelic disposition. Her Doctor frequently complained of dizziness and a rushing noise in the head. But as the winter wore on, he improved.

In March there came a messenger from Elector John. He brought a piece of fine, leather-colored cloth for a new cloak which Luther was to wear at the coming Diet of Augsburg in April. John asked his theologians to draw up for him articles containing statements of their faith. Kate sighed secretly as she read the letter. They were to hold themselves in readiness to accompany the Elector on his journey to Augsburg. That would mean a long absence again, she thought.

She was ready for it, however, and bade her husband a cheery farewell when he left on the third of April in the company of his old friends—Melanchthon, Jonas, and Spalatin. Another old friend who joined them was Agricola, who had recently moved to Wittenberg with his large family.

About a month later Kate received a message from Peter with the news that Luther's father had passed away after a long illness. Peter hoped that now he could come to Wittenberg to live with them.

The first letter Kate had from her Doctor told her that he had safely arrived in Coburg and preached there on

Easter Sunday. Then the others had gone on to Augsburg while he had been escorted to Coburg castle by the Elector's men.

"So," he wrote, "my dear Master Kate, my Morning Star of Wittenberg, beloved Doctoress, I am not to go to Augsburg because the Elector deems it unsafe for me. But he wants me near in case of need. Greetings to the whole household. How is my heart's dearest little Madge? And is little Hans a good boy? Does Tutor Weller have any trouble with him? Kate, my spectacles from Christian Doering are no good. Ask him to send me better ones. Tell my printers to get moving. If Weiss is afraid of printing a commentary on the Psalms, let George Rau publish it. It isn't right to give the devil a vacation. I have been given the prince's apartments and all his rooms. I live here like a prince myself. The castle is large and very high. It overlooks the whole town of Coburg and the view is beautiful. You should see the birds here, strutting about as if they owned the place, and whiling away heavy time with chattering. Last night I heard the first nightingale and it was a wonderful heavenly song. Nephew Cyriac Kaufmann is still here with me. He tells me that some thirty people take their meals here daily. If Jerome Weller tells me that Hans is good, I will send him a letter. Kiss Madge, Hans, Aunt Lena and yourself, my dear Kate. From your loving Martin."

Again he wrote: "I write much—every day—letters, tracts, translations of prophets. And now I have written several of Aesop's fables for my Germans, which I think will be of profit to them. I eat carefully. Yet, I have had a few of the old spells of faintness, dizziness, and suffering in body and mind. Now, too, the news of my good father's death grieves me deeply. Day and night I am occupied with examining Holy Scripture. Every word I turn over in my mind, meditate, and argue with myself. And more and more am I convinced of the truth of our doctrine, and more resolved, if God wills, never to allow another letter to be torn from us. Philip sometimes worries me. I have told him that 'faith cannot be found in rhetoric or philosophy. Faith must recognize the Supernatural and the Invisible and he who attempts to see and understand it receives only care and tears for his reward. The Lord said that He would dwell in the thick darkness.'

"Oh, Kate, my much beloved wife, I hope soon to be home with you and make music again. God keep you and the children. Greet Aunt Lena, my brother Peter, if he is already with you, and all the household."

Kate was relieved when finally in October he came home, after his six months' stay at the Coburg fortress. She boasted to him of the progress four-year-old Hans had made in his Latin study, with Jerome Weller to tutor him. How delighted she was when he called Hans, questioned him, then drew from the folds of his gown a beautiful marzipan booklet.

"Look at the youngster," he whispered to Kate, "look at him bite off a corner of his sugar book. It tastes better than Latin, I think. And now, Kate, show me my little Madge."

Chapter 11

Kate had won the battle for the extra piece of garden land she so badly wanted. It had cost her ninety gulden. Now she was dickering with Klaus Bildenhauer for a fish pond. She had told her Doctor so much about the carp, bass, pike, and trout that this pond would supply that he had begun to weaken. She had pointed out how beneficial for his health would be a little fishing now and then. Especially, since the recent death of his mother had saddened him. She had not long outlived Luther's father, and Peter had postponed his coming until later.

Kate had been patient and quiet during the time of his mother's illness. She was glad he had written her such a tender letter and glad that he had dedicated to her his book, *Pertaining to the Love of God.* But now she was determined to see action. She wanted that fish pond before someone else snatched it from her. She talked "fish pond" so incessantly that Luther asked her, "Kate, dear, did you say a prayer before your sermon?"

Ignoring his pointed question, she went on, "Doctor, I'll have the horse hitched to the little wagon if you'll drive out with me to look at it."

He threw up his hands. "Where will we get the money to pay for it?"

"Oh, it's only nine hundred gulden. I can manage that all right. And think of the large house that is part of the property. We might use that some day."

He shook his head. "Kate, will you ever get through planning?"

"But Doctor," she countered impatiently, "we need it. You like fish. Everybody likes fish. I have to have fish now and then to feed all those people at our table. Would you rather have me buy them, fish by fish, at the market and spend a thousand gulden?"

She saw him smile and knew that he was amused. She had the horse hitched to the light basket carriage and after dinner they drove out to look at their prospective property. Bildenhauer talked and explained, praising his fish. Kate enthusiastically chimed in. She could see herself winning.

"Well," her Doctor sighed at last, "I don't see how I can hold the fort any longer. My Kate is determined. Oh, well, why should I worry? Kate pays the bills. She can strike fire from nothing."

So the deal was closed. Kate handed over the money and drove home with her Doctor in high spirits.

"Well, Master Kate," he began as they drove along at a brisk trot, "now you have everything your heart desires—your cloister garden with the brewhouse, your out-of-town garden, your fish pool, your kitchen renovated, your storeroom, your bathroom, your laundry, your cells upstairs all furnished with cots . . ." he paused to draw a deep breath and looked at her comically, "your two women servants, your swineherd to guard the pigs, and a stableman who is king over the barnyard populace—the chickens, ducks, geese, and the old proud peacock who struts around as if the whole world belonged to him. And I have my man Wolf. Why, Kate, we have a household like the rich."

Kate flipped the reins and urged the horse on to a swift canter. "And at that, dear Doctor," she said, "you forgot to mention my orchard."

"I helped you with that, Kate, didn't I? How are all the fruit trees doing?"

Kate raised her head proudly. "There will be peaches, pears, apples aplenty according to the looks of it. The cherries are already gone. Then there is the mulberry coming, and I saw a few figs on the tree I planted last year."

"Figs," Luther sniffed, "I don't think I'll care for them."

"But you will learn," Kate said. "They are very, very sweet. I tasted one at the Cranachs. But that was dried and came from afar."

"And the grapevine?"

"That, too, is bearing. I expect to make wine and dry some grapes for the winter."

He said nothing and for a while they drove on in silence. "You worry me sometimes," he now remarked quietly.

"Why?"

"I'm afraid, Kate, that you're trying to make your paradise on earth."

"But, Doctor! God gave us all these fruits and flowers and vegetables and trees! Surely, He doesn't want us to sit in tears all day long."

"Kate!" she recognized that intonation of impatience in his voice, "you know that God wants us to be happy—to 'rejoice in the Lord.' Yes, we can laugh and be merry and enjoy all the good things God showers on us, but there is still great danger of becoming worldly. Heaven, after all, is our goal."

Kate sighed. "I'm afraid," she said contritely, "that I am naturally worldly. I do love this beautiful world and everything that's in it."

At this he burst into laughter. "Truly, you are the old Eve over and over. But seriously, Kate, I hope you're through planning now."

Kate gazed into the distance intently. Then she turned her head a bit and, looking at him, said coyly, "No, there's one more thing, my beloved Doctor."

He did not answer and she sensed that he was really annoyed. So she quickly added, "There's just one more thing. But that will come later."

As they drove into the cloister grounds which Kate had turned into a beauty spot, he turned to her solicitously, "You shouldn't overdo, Kate, because of the little one coming soon."

She laughed carelessly. "I'm strong and I like to work. And I hope this little one will be a boy and come on your birthday, so we can have a big celebration."

Her wish was almost fulfilled. She was given a chance to harvest all her fruit, to dry and store away some, to bury root vegetables in the cellar, to make wine, to brew beer, to clean and bake, to chop and mince, and knit and sew. The new baby, a boy, obligingly came on November 9 and was named Martin, after his father. And as with the others, there was a baptismal celebration. Peter, with his happy smile, was one of the proud sponsors.

Kate had little time for herself. With three children to care for, a husband who had frequent ailments, and an ever-increasing household to provide for, she could rarely pause long enough to catch her breath. When things became too hectic, she would spend an afternoon with her beloved Katy Jonas.

Luther and his associates—Melanchthon, Justus Jonas, Bugenhagen, Roerer and Cruciger—still labored daily over the Bible translation. When her Doctor complained that the Hebrew of the Old Testament was so much more difficult to translate than the New Testament Greek, Kate listened thoughtfully.

"You are the first one," she said, "not to translate from the Latin Vulgate. Surely such a painstaking translation must receive God's blessing. Your 'Sanhedrin' has sometimes spent three days on one word."

"Yes," he nodded, "it is necessary that we all work together, compare opinions, and finally come to a decision. The only one who sways me sometimes," he added playfully, "is Roerer."

Kate laughed mischievously. "The way I do?"

"Yes, the way you do. You see, Kate, Aaron had just one Moses to dominate him, but I have three: Roerer, Master Kate, and Wolf."

This brought a chuckle from Kate. Then, sobering, she asked, "How much longer will it take to complete the work?"

"If all goes well, we might finish next year. Elector John is anxious to see it in print."

Elector John, however, did not live to see it printed. He died before the year was over. His son, John Frederick, a worthy successor of his father, John, and of his uncle, Frederick, was present at the great dinner Kate gave in honor of the occasion.

John Frederick lifted the heavy volume, which numbered 908 pages, for all to see. "This book," he said, "we should hold most precious. It has meant twelve or more years of the combined labor of at least half a dozen men. Hans Lufft, who printed it, now has a claim to fame. His name will be remembered."

During the animated conversation that followed, Kate quietly slipped out of the room. She was back a little later, carrying her newest baby, a chubby four-month-old, on her arm.

"Elector John Frederick," she exclaimed, proudly standing before him, "this is our little Paul. He came just in time for this celebration."

The Elector took the baby from her arms and fondled him. Little Paul examined the bearded face carefully, then smiled and cooed happily.

John Frederick handed him back to his mother. "A fine child," he said, "he will grow up to be a great man some day like his father. I heard about your Hans and Madeline and Martin from my father and my uncle. God bless them all!" he added, helping himself to the sweets and fruit that were being passed.

Kate long remembered this day. The words of the

Elector kept ringing in her ears. Little Paul, with his rosy cheeks, was a splendid specimen of humanity. Perhaps he would . . . At this point in her thoughts she always checked herself. Her Doctor would not like such worldly, ambitious planning. He called it vanity.

Kate had a sense of guilt when she thought of her many "vanities"—her ambitious planning for the house and for the children's future. How could she harbor such fancies when her Doctor was undergoing such anguish again? Although he jested and spoke lightly of his headaches and dizziness, she could see that his appetite was poor.

She knew that the ever-widening rift between him and Erasmus grieved him deeply. While Erasmus expressed the "highest respect" for Luther's scholarship, his timid soul took fright at the Reformer's heroic decisiveness and vehemence. He contended that Luther was bringing ruin and anarchy to the church. Bitter and violent letters were exchanged between them which, Kate knew, must end in complete enmity.

Henry VIII also was a source of trouble. Previously he had written Luther pious letters and even sent a gift of several hundred gulden. When Henry saw that Luther could not be "bought" to espouse his divorce from Catherine, he wrote coarse, insulting letters.

Kate forgot all about her personal ambitions when she realized how these matters were wearing down her Doctor's health. The climax came when he told her that Dr. Glatz, her despised former lover, had turned against the church. When he had finished relating this story, he collapsed at her feet. Fortunately Peter came in just then. Together they carried him to his room. Peter hurried to call the physician, Melanchthon, Agricola, and Veit Dietrich. Physician Schurf came and, after examining the patient, took Kate aside and whispered, "It looks as if a stroke might take him."

Kate spent the night with him alone—watching, praying, and nursing him. "Hot cloths," Schurf had said. "Always keep him warm. Give him his medicine promptly." She did all that and more. Peter shared her anxiety and kept peeping in at the door. Toward morning she whispered to Peter that she could see he was improving.

His recovery was slow. For days afterward he remained weak. Then a message came from Hans Loeser with an invitation to join the Elector's hunting party within a few days. The winter air, the exercise outdoors would do him an immense lot of good, they reasoned. Luther hesitated at first, then gave in to Kate and Aunt Lena's entreaty.

When he came home with a huge piece of wild boar, Kate was dumbfounded. All the family came crowding around him.

"Oh, Doctor," Kate greeted him, "you look much better. And did you really join the hunters?"

"Doesn't it look like it?" he jested, exhibiting the boar meat. "Tomorrow, my Kate, you shall cook this wild boar for us. And here is a jug of wine John Frederick sent to go with it."

Kate still looked unconvinced. She knew her Doctor. "Did you . . . really . . ."

"Yes, I went out with the hunters, but stayed by myself. And what do you think happened?"

She shook her head.

Then he went on, "A little white rabbit, frightened out of his wits by pursuing dogs, stormed at me and I hid him in the folds of my cloak."

"Oh!"

"And did you kill him, Father?" asked young Hans, wide-eyed with interest. Little Madge tugged at her father's leg and repeated innocently, "Kill him?"

Luther patted his son's shoulder, caught his little daughter up in his arms and kissed her affectionately. "No, Hans," he said, "I couldn't hurt the little creature. He was trembling with fright. I held him close and when the dogs were gone, I let him go."

"That is just like you, Martin," Aunt Lena put in, "you're always kind."

"Was that all?" Kate asked.

"No. Much more happened. After that, I took my Bible and climbed back into the wagon and began to translate Psalm 147. That is my booty—the best of all. As soon as it is printed, I shall send Hans Loeser a copy. Now that is what I call great hunting. It takes from no one and gives to everyone."

Little Madge kept her arms around her father's neck and, when he attempted to put her down, she kissed him and held him all the tighter.

"Heart's dearest child," he said, "I must get back to work. But first, we'll take a peep at baby Paul. How do you like your little brother?"

"Love him," she said earnestly, "he's angel."

Kate, who followed them to the crib, saw his eyes grow moist. There was softness in them as he turned to look at her. "She's an angel herself, that dear little Madge," he said, in an undertone. "Never gives any trouble like Hans. Does she?"

"Oh, Doctor," Kate was quick to defend her eldest, "Hans is good, too. But he is a boy."

"Do you think that gives him more right to be naughty?"

"N-no, but . . ."

"So Paul sleeps and eats well?"

"Yes, isn't he the picture of health?"

He set Madge down on the floor and, with a last pat, said, "Now I must go. Tonight, after supper, we will sing and play if mother lets you stay up a while." He kissed her once more and walked away. Her eyes followed him as long as she could see him. Then, childlike, she gave a gleeful squeal and ran to meet Mrs. Jonas whom she saw coming into the room. Halfway across the room she stopped to pick up a doll.

"My!" Katy Jonas commented, after exchanging greetings with Kate, "what a sweet, lovable child. And how she loves her father," she added, putting down her sewing. "I saw the look in her eyes."

Kate brought her sewing and motioned Katy to be seated in her favorite window niche. "Yes, and her father loves her so, too. I wish he'd feel the same way toward Hans. But I don't think he'll ever love his boys like Madge."

"Well," said Katy Jonas in her light way, "I wouldn't

worry about it. Your Hans is a little harder to handle and . . ." casting Kate a quick look, "maybe he's a little spoiled, too."

Both looked up when the door opened and in came gaunt Wolf followed by Hans and the crouching Toelpel. The big fellow grinned when the boy ran to his mother, held up a tangled mesh and shouted, "Look what Wolf made for me!"

Kate frowned. "What is it?"

"Nets," Hans said triumphantly. "Nets. So I can catch the birds in spring."

Kate's eyes flashed angrily. Her voice was stern. "Wolf," she said, "is that all you have to do—make nets to catch the birds?" She took the nets from Hans, who protested loudly. "No, you shall not have them. You shall not catch little birds in nets. Wolf," turning to the elder offender, "how can you be so cruel? And don't you know that Doctor Luther has forbidden you to ever hurt a single little bird or animal?"

The big man with the childish face hung his head in shame, Toelpel cringed at his feet and, when Wolf started for the door, slunk after him. Then Kate turned her attention to her son.

"Go, Hans," she said severely, "get your Latin book and study, so that Jerome Weller doesn't tell your father you don't know anything."

Hans obeyed reluctantly. Coming back with his book balancing on his head, he dropped it on the floor. When Madge darted into his path and picked up his book, he tore it away from her, shouting rudely. Kate called Madge, took her on her lap, then whispered to Katy Jonas, "Don't pay any attention to him." Then aloud, "Will you stay for supper?"

Katy Jonas smiled and fidgeted with her sewing. "Oh, I'd love to, but do you think we ought to? We're here so often and you always have so many at your table."

"That'll be all the merrier," Kate said. "And I baked some fine wheat bread today that you'll like. And a cake with sugar. You know it isn't often that you can buy a loaf of sugar. And we'll have fresh fried fish . . ."

"Stop!" Katy Jonas laughed. "I can't resist that. It sounds good enough for the Elector himself."

"The Elector sent a piece of wild boar along with Doctor," Kate rambled on, "we'll have that tomorrow noon."

"I don't see how you manage to feed all these people," Katy marveled. "How many are there at your table now?"

Kate counted. "There are about half a dozen nieces and nephews, a dozen student boarders, and often Master Philip or Bugenhagen or Roerer, and you can always be sure of one or two just dropping in."

"Oh, Kate, you are wonderful!"

"I have help," Kate replied nonchalantly. She looked over her sewing at her son who was now busy with his book and, putting Madge down, she rose saying she must see how Hannah and Dorothy were getting along with the fish.

"And here comes Aunt Lena now with baby Paul," she remarked, "and he's still tired and rubbing his eyes. Well, Katy, they'll keep you company."

When, a little later, she reappeared to announce supper, she found the baby on Katy's lap, Madge on her aunt's lap, Hans kneeling on the floor listening to one of Aunt Lena's stories. Kate hurried away again to help the servants dish up. Already the supper party was beginning to assemble and Kate could see by their animated conversation that this was going to be an interesting meal. Luther was in high spirits. When Madge came running to him, he lifted her up on his arm and called her his "heart's dearest." Kate had her sit between them, and Hans on her other side. Next to Hans sat Aunt Lena who had handed the baby over to one of the nieces. Melanchthon and Justus and Katy Jonas sat on the other side of their host.

Luther gave the signal for them to fold their hands and bow their heads in prayer. Hans followed with his prayer, and Madge prompted by her father, stammered her little verse. Then all were seated and a buzz of conversation filled the room. Kate looked the length of the table and shook her head disapprovingly. Too much talking!

"Folks," her clear voice broke sharply into the babble, "stop talking! Start eating. Don't let my fish spoil and get cold. They have to be eaten crisp and hot."

The color rose to her face as she caught her Doctor's significant smile. "Yes, folks," he repeated earnestly, "don't let the food get cold! My 'Morning Star' would not like that. And, after all—she works hard. And these fish are from her own pond. They are very special."

"They are special," Katy Jonas agreed. "They are the best fish I've ever eaten."

Luther put a piece on his plate, helped Madge to some, and remarked, "Kate gets so much fun out of her fish pond, and why shouldn't we enjoy them if our Lord puts these pike and carp in the lake for us. No harm in a glass of beer or Rhine wine with it. God wants us to be happy and to laugh."

While the fish platter was being replenished by Hannah, Dorothy came in with a huge bowl of cottage cheese. This was one of Kate's specialties. She herself poured the beer with sparing hand. She was always careful not to overdo food and drink. Kate, her Doctor, and the most distinguished guests used heavy silver forks, still a novelty, given her by an Italian friend. The students and others used fingers and bread crusts as pushers.

The noise of eating was undisturbed for several moments until Luther, looking up, called jocularly, "Well, you prelates, what's the news? What's going on here, there, and everywhere? Who knows something?"

The younger men exchanged glances and nudged one another. Finally, one of them spoke up, "It may not be new any more, but it was interesting to me to find in the geographical book written by Waldseemoeller that the New World is called *America.*"

All looked interested. "It seems sure now," Melanchthon said, "that this name will be permanent."

"But why America? Why not Columbia?" another student asked.

The first one replied, "Because Americus Vespucius

made several voyages and wrote letters about the new country."

"And now," Luther said, "there is much exploring going on among the English, the Dutch, the French, and the Spanish."

"They are all looking for gold," Justus Jonas put in.

"What became of Columbus?" Kate asked. "Is he still living?"

No one knew. Finally, a foreigner, an exiled priest from Spain, said in Latin, "He died dishonored and of a broken heart."

Luther said with an air of finality, "We all know that the Bible says, 'Put not your trust in princes,' and 'Seek not riches.' "

"But, Doctor," Kate remonstrated, "you have to have money to live. Else you can't pay your debts. And I still think," she added emphatically, "that you should not do all your writing and lecturing without pay. Do you not think so, Master Philip?"

Melanchthon half nodded and looked at Luther. The students vigorously applauded. Several shouted, "Mrs. Luther is right!" Then Luther spoke.

"The church has grown mercenary," he said, "during all these centuries. The clergy is after money as much as the princes and nobles. Now it behooves us to show the world that a Christian can afford to do things without pay for every hand's turn."

"Good words," approved Jerome Weller.

Kate, alone, was unconvinced. "You men can speak easily and nobly about not accepting any money when all you have to do is to sit down at a good table and eat. But we women must see to it that there is something to put on the table. And we need money for clothes. The children cannot go in rags. And the servants must be paid promptly."

Luther's eyes sparkled. "We must have faith, dear Kate," he said. "Faith, though it sees and understands nothing, yet trusts in the Lord in everything. The faith that Moses had when he led Israel out of Egypt. The faith that Abraham had when he led Isaac away to sacrifice him."

There was a murmur of approval, then Kate said boldly, "I never could see how God could ask such a thing of Abraham—to offer his own son! And, Doctor, I can't understand either how Abraham could even think of doing it!"

He reached across Madge, and patted Kate's arm. "You need not understand, dear Kate. Only believe. Trust. The Lord said that He will 'dwell in the thick darkness.' And He is ever ready to help—with money, with silver cups, with food, with drink, with clothes, with anything that we may need. Now," he concluded, "shall we rise and pray? It is too late to sing more than one song now."

After the meal, some went to their rooms. Others stood about talking or went for a walk before going to the chapel where Luther preached and held a short service. Kate went with the Justus Jonases. When she and her Doctor returned, the house was quiet. Aunt Lena had retired after putting the children to bed. The servants and student boarders were in their own rooms.

The great living-room was cozy in the soft candlelight. The tile stove spread warmth all around. Kate, the night owl as well as the morning star, was in a mood to stay up and chat. But her Doctor was tired and had turned to go to his room when Wolf ushered in a messenger with a note.

Kate took it to her husband and they read it together. It was from a pastor's widow with a request that Luther find her a husband since she felt so lonely. Luther went out to see the messenger.

"Tell the lady," he said, "that I am very sorry I can do nothing for her. She is of age and must look out for herself."

With this he dismissed the disappointed man. Then, turning to Kate, who could not hide her amusement, he laughed, "They must think I run a matrimonial agency, besides all the other things I do."

Kate caught his arm and squeezed it. "You are so kind and helpful, dear Doctor, so everyone tries to get something out of you for nothing."

Chapter 12

When Aunt Lena emerged from Kate's bedroom that December morning, carrying a white bundle, she walked straight up to the Doctor and put it into his arms.

"A daughter," she whispered, loosening the cover so as to let him get a peep at the infant. He gazed at the mite, then asked in an anxious undertone, "And Kate?"

"As well as any woman can be after going through that ordeal," Aunt Lena said. "She's sleeping now and should not be disturbed."

"Thank heaven all is well!" he sighed, greatly relieved. "And thank heaven, too, for this lovely gift." He looked at the babe with new interest, still holding her in his arms. "Aunt Lena," he went on, "I am a rich man. Each child is worth more than a whole kingdom to me. And I now have five kingdoms."

Aunt Lena took the bundle from him, remarking, "If you hadn't lost baby Elizabeth, you would now have six kingdoms. Yes, dear Martin, you are rich with your five children and your devoted wife."

"Nothing lovelier than a woman's love. My beloved

Mrs. Cotta told me that often. And I love my Kate more than I can say. Now I will go and bring the children to look at their new sister."

He soon returned, carrying two-year-old Paul on his arm. Martin, now about three, and Madge a little over five, had hold of his other hand. Eight-year-old Hans brought up the rear with his usual bravado.

"Where is my new sister?" he demanded. "Aunt Lena, is that my sister?" He began tugging at the white bundle and, when Aunt Lena sat down, lowering it to her knees and carefully opening it a bit, he gazed critically.

"She's real red," he commented, "and she hasn't any hair. Look, Madge, isn't she funny?"

Little Madge peered at the infant in the covers with great, innocent eyes. She tugged at her father's hand and looked at him questioningly, "Do you like her, Father? Do you think she is a nice sister for me?"

He nodded as he held up Paul for a glimpse. "Yes, dear Madge," he assured her, "God sent you a nice little sister to love and to play with."

Martin crowded closer. "I want to see my sister, too. Can she play with me?"

"When she is bigger," his father explained. "Now she's tiny and helpless."

The baby screwed up her face and began to fumble with her tiny hands.

"Now she's redder than ever," Hans laughed.

"Come, Hans," Luther took hold of his son's arm, "it's time for you to get back to your Latin with Tutor Weller. Now, go."

"Father," Madge pleaded, "do I have to go, too? I know all my Latin."

He set Paul down and bent lower to kiss Madge. "You help Aunt Lena take care of these two brothers and play quietly so you don't disturb your mother."

"Is Mother sick?"

"She is weak, dear child, since God put the new baby in her arms. She needs rest. So you must be my good little daughter."

"I will, Father." She clung to his hand for a moment and kissed it with childlike devotion. Then, with a pat for Martin and Paul, he went out.

Kate called, "Aunt Lena, bring me the baby." When the infant was at her side, Kate asked, "And the other children? I heard Doctor take Hans out. Was he naughty again?" she asked weakly.

"No, Katykin," Aunt Lena mothered, "he's just a wide-awake boy and a little mischievous. But Martin was afraid he might disturb you."

Kate put her free arm over the child lightly. "Aunt Lena," she murmured, "I love this little one dearly, like all the others. And I thank God for them all. As soon as I'm stronger, I'll work again. I have many plans."

She thought she saw a smile flit over Aunt Lena's dear old face as she replied softly, "Yes, but now you must rest, good child. And I'll see what the children are doing. You know, Madge takes it so seriously when her father tells her to watch the boys." She moved toward the door. "And I'll see what Dorothy and Hannah are doing. I'll bring you a good, warm beer soup. That will strengthen you."

Kate closed her eyes contentedly. What a privileged woman she was, she thought. A husband with a heart of pure gold and five lovely children. Only one they had to give up. Some people lost two or three. And good Aunt Lena, a real mother and grandmother. So many good friends. Dependable servants. A good home—a happy, sunny home. Of course, it wasn't all sunshine. There were storms and sickness and sadness, she mused. That was a part of everybody's life. But being Christians, as the Apostle Paul said, you could "rejoice in the Lord always." Her Doctor said that Christians could be walking amid roses at all times, even when bowed down by a heavy cross.

So, in spite of all the adversities her Doctor had to contend with, the wranglings and disagreements, his frequent illnesses and weak spells, his spiritual sufferings, his disappointments, they were very happy. Even though he still gave away precious cups and needed gulden, they had never suffered from lack of anything. It always came back to them in some way.

"God is rich," Kate mused, "just as Doctor always tells me. Otherwise, I do not see how we run this big household with five children, half a dozen poor nieces and nephews, students and boarders who can't pay for anything, daily dinner guests. Then the big dinners I have to give, the gifts for sponsors, weddings, beggars and so on. Well, last year I made a few extra gulden selling pigs, chickens, eggs, and vegetables." She suddenly felt exhausted and lay back with closed eyes. She glowed with happiness when she heard her children in the adjoining room playing with Mietzi, the cat. Madge's gentle voice kept exhorting the two small boys to play quietly so that mother could rest.

Rest! That was the last thing Kate wanted to do. She was impatient, driven by a hundred duties and plans. Christmas was almost upon them with more work than ever to do. Elsie von Kanitz had promised them a visit between the holidays. The son of Mrs. von Cotta was coming about the same time. He would stay indefinitely. He might bring his wife. Kate wanted to do all she possibly could for Cotta because his mother had given a home to her Doctor when he was a forsaken boy. Kate's gratitude toward the Cottas was endless.

She left her bed before the tenth day and helped prepare the baptismal dinner. She helped with the Christmas doings. In February a sister of her Doctor arrived, bringing two orphaned nieces with her. They were to stay until they married or found suitable employment. She already had nine nephews and nieces besides her own five children to take care of. But she accepted these as graciously as she did all that came to her for help. More than before she now depended on Peter's cheerful assistance. Besides attending lectures he earned his keep by making himself generally useful. Frequently he took the children off her hands, worked in the stables, helped with gardening, and did much marketing.

Among the important new visitors at the University this year were several Englishmen. They had come to see

Luther and to study his reforms. The Luthers immediately liked Dr. Barnes because of his sincere religious interests.

His soft-spoken manner and kind smile took the children by storm. Hans admired the little green feather in his velvet beret. Madge liked him for the English words he taught her. Martin and Paul followed him about the room and tried to sit near him.

Barnes told them about Henry VIII and his headstrong actions. He had crushed Wolsey, broken with the pope, made himself head of the church and persecuted Catholics and Protestants alike. The blood on the executioner's axe was never dry these days. The whole trouble revolved around Catherine, who had been Henry's brother's wife before he married her. Of the five sickly children she had borne him only a daughter remained. Henry was determined to put Catherine aside and marry Anne Boleyn.

Barnes became a daily guest at Kate's table during his stay. She invited him for the dinner she gave when Bugenhagen received his doctor's degree. He was there again when Hans's tutor, Jerome Weller, was given his degree as doctor of divinity.

Soon after Barnes left, sickness invaded the home. Luther was plagued with headaches and dizziness. He next had an attack of gallstones. In his despair he asked Kate for a dish of split peas and fried herring with mustard. When Dr. Schurf arrived he found Luther eating this dish. His joking explanation was that eating it had cured him. Soon after this, measles broke out among the students, and in the summer the pest paid a return visit to Wittenberg.

Again most of the people of the University fled the city. John Frederick sent Luther a letter urging him to leave also. But Luther scoffed at this fear, saying, "They have no faith. In fact, some of them caught ulcers in their pockets; others colic in their books and gout in their papers." He told Kate that much more was known about the "great plague in Wittenberg" in other places than in Wittenberg itself.

"It proves," he said, "how much bigger and fatter lies grow the farther they travel." Actually, he and Kate knew of only a few cases of the plague. They were greatly relieved, however, when talk about it subsided and the University took up life as usual.

The summer faded away. Kate had once again harvested, stored, and disposed of her great supply of vegetables and fruits. But she had been tired often. Baby Margaret, who would be a year old on the seventeenth of December, demanded much attention. She liked to be rocked to sleep. Kate had no time for this, being overloaded with other work. Aunt Lena could not be spared. Peter was busy around the house. The two small boys couldn't be trusted with the baby and Hans and Madge were with their tutor.

One morning in particular when the baby persisted in crying, a distraught Kate burst into her husband's study. "Oh, Doctor," she cried, "I'm almost beside myself! So much to do before Christmas. So many people coming. All those children to look after and the little one yelling her head off—couldn't you take care of her for me?"

Kate was too excited to notice the surprised look on

her husband's face. She drew a relieved sigh when he quickly rose and said, "Why, yes, dear Kate. I'll come this minute and take care of Margaret. Go about your work in peace."

She waited only long enough to see him pick up his lute and a bunch of papers. He followed her to the big living-room and then disappeared into the bedroom. Now, at last, she was free to work undisturbed. So absorbed did she become that she heeded nothing and took no notice of the stillness that had settled on the house. With a sudden start, she remembered that she had left baby Margaret in charge of her Doctor, and that the two smaller boys had been playing in the living-room. She must see what they were doing. Leaving the fruit she had been cutting up for a sweet bread, she hurried to the bedroom. All was quiet. The children in the living-room were looking at a picture book with Madge. "The dear child," Kate thought, as she hurried by, "I can always depend on Madge to take care of the smaller children when she's through with her own lessons."

She listened for a moment at the closed bedroom door, then cautiously opened it a trifle just as her Doctor reached for his lute. He had rocked the baby to sleep and now began to pick a few notes on the lute—softly, softly, so as not to waken the little one. What she heard sounded so sweet to Kate's ears that the stood still on the threshold, touching a corner of her apron to her eyes.

He saw her then.

"Kate," he said, picking up a paper from a nearby table, "I had an inspiration. While sitting here, rocking my little child, I thought of the Christ child coming down from heaven for us sinners. Listen."

She let herself drop into a chair while he began to read:

> Good news from heaven the angels bring,
> Glad tidings to the earth they sing:
> To us this day a Child is given
> To crown us with the joy of heaven.

Reverently he read through twelve verses and, reverently, with bowed head, Kate listened. Then he came to the thirteenth verse—*Ach, mein herzliebstes Jesulein:*

> Ah, dearest Jesus, Holy Child,
> Make Thee a bed, soft, undefiled,
> Within my heart, that it may be
> A quiet chamber kept for Thee.

Kate covered her face with both hands to hide the tears that were raining from her eyes. When he had finished the fifteenth verse, he turned to her, tenderness in his eyes.

"You are not crying, my Kate?"

Quickly she brushed her damp hands against her apron. "No," she choked, taking his hand and squeezing it, "no, why should I cry when you make up such a beautiful cradle song for the dear Christ child? No wonder my little one went to sleep. But now," she added, withdrawing her hand, "how about the music for it? I think you have it already."

His eyes were luminous. "Yes, I have it already and will teach it to the household as soon as I can develop it sufficiently. Listen, Kate," as he picked up his lute.

Quite overcome, Kate could only nod her approval. "Perhaps soon—this Christmas Eve—we can sing it in church," she suggested. "We need more songs. If you'll teach the children . . . Oh, here comes Madge."

"Dear Father!" She snuggled up to Luther and, looking into his face, pleaded, "Please, Father, sing that again about the Holy Child. It sounded so good."

Kate knew he couldn't resist Madge. She saw him quickly kiss the top of Madge's fair hair and stroke her cheek. Then, reaching for his lute, he said, "I will sing but one verse, for it is a long song and we will begin to practice it tonight." And he began again:

Ah, dearest Jesus, Holy Child . . .

When he had finished, Madge said, "I think the Holy Child will like it if we sing it Christmas Eve."

They practiced that evening after supper. Melanchthon was there and several students. Hans sang with all his heart. Madge sang with her sweet clear voice, always watching her father with bright eyes. Paul on his mother's lap tried to join in, and Martin on Aunt Lena's lap, was fast learning the verses and the melody. He was four now and already learning Latin. Only on rare occasions would he submit to Aunt Lena's lap. Jonas and his Katy dropped in for a short time, adding their voices to the others.

Soon after seven the little singing circle broke up, for the children must get to bed. Melanchthon promised to come again the following evening and bring his son, Philip. Maybe his wife would come also. The Jonases would surely come again and bring their Justus. The students would bring other students. They would all practice and be ready to sing the song on Christmas Eve. In that way the entire congregation would soon learn it.

Kate's ears rang for days after with the songs they were all singing and with the happy prattle of the children. The household was alive with the Christmas spirit. Giving —loving! Who ever gave more than the Christ child? Who could love as much as the Christ child? Kate went frequently out to the market or to one of the shops to look for some appropriate gift for each one in the family, for the servants, and for special friends and godchildren.

"Will the Christ child bring me something?" Martin asked every day.

"If you say your prayers and are a good boy," Kate told him, "there'll be something for you."

"Me, too?" Paul pleaded. "I can pray." With that he folded his hands and gave a demonstration of his praying ability, so that Kate was deeply touched.

"Always remember," she told them earnestly, "it isn't gifts alone that should make us happy at Christmas time. It is the dear Christ child who loved us so much that He came down to earth."

"Yes," Hans nodded sagely, "to be crucified and buried for us."

"I wish I could have seen him," Madge murmured with shining eyes. Then she broke into:

Ah, dearest Jesus, Holy Child,
Make Thee a bed, soft, undefiled . . .

The other children automatically joined in, and, when they had finished the last verse, Kate admonished, "Now we must not disappoint the Christ child. We must all do our best."

"Then he mustn't disappoint us, either," Hans said critically. "He must send us snow."

"When will the snow come?" Martin wanted to know.

"We have to watch for it," Madge explained, "every day till Christmas. From today on, it's ten more days."

"Ten more days," Martin said.

Nine more days, and no snow. Eight days—first snow, beautiful, glittering white snow. The children crowded into Kate's favorite window niche to watch it come down. Thicker and thicker it fell. Bigger and bigger the flakes grew. By the time they went to bed everything was covered with a heavy white layer. The next morning it was still snowing. Peter went out and made a great snowman. Kate and the children watched him from the window as he fashioned the monster. He gave him a carrot nose, stuck two pieces of rounded blue crockery into the hollowed eye sockets and a piece of burnt wood for a mustache. Wolf brought him a discarded hat with a chicken feather and a heavy club to hold in his arms.

Then the two stood surveying their masterpiece with evident gratification and the children, all bundled up, came out to dance around the snowman. Madge had found black buttons with which she added the finishing touch.

Even Luther joined in the general merriment. He named the snowman *Pelznickel.*[1] So, watching and joking about old *Pelznickel,* they lost count of the days till, one morning, Madge said: "Tonight is Christmas Eve. And we will sing Father's song 'From Heaven Above.' "

---

[1] St. Nicholas dressed in furs.

After the service, Kate gathered her little brood and her household around the festive table in the living-room. The two tall candles spread a warm glow over the gifts, toys, fruits, sweets, nuts, and marzipan arranged there. The little ones crowed with delight. The servants were all there, waiting to receive their gifts—Wolf, Hannah, Dorothy, the stableman, the swineherd, and one or two others irregularly employed; and also the orphaned nieces, nephews, and Peter.

"But where is your father?" Kate asked, turning to Hans. "We can't distribute gifts until he is here."

Hans ran to the door, Madge at his heels. "He's coming now," he cried, opening the door and peering down the dimly-lit circular stairway, "I hear him. Oh," he added laughingly, "he's all white like *Pelznickel!*"

Kate handed the baby to Aunt Lena and ran to the door to see for herself. There was her Doctor just as Hans had said, "all white," covered with snow. Gasping and laughing merrily he climbed the stairs.

"Get started, Kate," Luther said. "Meanwhile, Hans can get my lute so that we can sing a few songs."

Wolf was first on the list with a woolen shawl, for which he was very thankful. Hannah and Dorothy were given warm cloth for winter dresses. The stableman and the swineherd received knitted mittens. Peter was happy about a traveling bag. The nieces and nephews received small gifts. For Hans there was a new book. Madge hugged a handsome doll. Paul was trying his hobbyhorse and Martin examined a Noah's Ark. Aunt Lena was happy about a new white ruching from Kate. She had given each of the children a small trinket and placed a bowl of rare fruit on the table. Kate gave her Doctor a picture of the Virgin with her Babe. He gave her a rare potted plant.

Kate invited the servants to help themselves to the nuts and sweets on the table. Then Luther picked up his lute and they sang once more "From Heaven Above." Next Kate suggested her favorite, "In Dulci Jubilo." Madge wanted "O Come, Immanuel." Several others were sung, then, with a prayer, the servants were dismissed. Only Wolf stayed. He helped Paul try out his hobby-horse and showed Martin how to set up his animals. Aunt Lena and Hans retired to a corner to read the new book. Kate busied herself about the room.

"Look at *Pelznickel!*" Madge exclaimed, going to the window. "He's still there and oh! the moon is shining right down on him."

Chapter 13

Peter's place at the table was empty. He had left one morning early in the spring for the Holy Land. For years he had saved money and planned to make this journey with an old friend. Once the day of departure was set, nothing that Luther or Kate said to dissuade him from this dangerous undertaking could move Peter. He merely smiled patiently and told them that the traveling bag they had given him for Christmas was packed.

They bade him farewell and wished him God's blessing on his way. The children cried and clung to him. When they were out of hearing, Kate turned to her Doctor with a sigh. "Good old Peter! We'll never see him again. I have a feeling."

Luther shrugged. "Only God knows."

They had no time to bemoan his going, for a great surprise awaited them. Early in the summer their old friend, Dr. Robert Barnes, paid them an unexpected visit. He had come directly from England bringing with him Bishop Edward Fox and Archdeacon Richard Heath. Henry VIII, who had definitely turned Protestant and married Anne Boleyn, now sent this committee "in the matters of the gospel."

Succumbing to her curiosity Kate asked Barnes, "And how is the marriage going?"

"There's much merrymaking every day," Barnes told her. "The King seems happy and is hoping that Anne's child will be the much-desired son."

"And if it isn't?"

Barnes shook his head. "Then may God protect Anne. No one else can."

It was evident that the subject was distasteful to him and that he thought nothing of Henry's religion, whether Protestant or Catholic. Kate pressed the matter no further. She was planning a banquet for the Englishmen and was head over heels in other work. Since the Agricolas with their nine children had moved in with them because they could find no other place in Wittenberg, there were eleven more mouths to feed.

"Those Agricolas!" Kate thought. If only Peter were here now to shepherd that swarm of children. They were so puny that even her wholesome food might not be enough to make them grow stronger. Kate's heart went out to pale, self-effacing Mrs. Agricola, whom she affectionately called "Grikel." Kate longed to breathe a little life into the sweet, dear soul.

Master Agricola found no such favor in Kate's eyes. From her Doctor she learned that there had been differences between the two men previously. Before coming here, Agricola had been stationed at Eisleben in the service of Count Albert of Mansfeld. His eccentricities in the matter of discipline had caused great dissatisfaction there. When reproved, he rudely quit the service. Count Albert denounced him as a "dangerous" individual. Nevertheless Luther had welcomed him back to Wittenberg. He had gotten him the position as teacher at the University with a good salary. Agricola was even permitted to preach.

Kate predicted trouble sooner or later. "That cynical smile," she said to her Doctor, "those prying eyes and sharp features . . ."

"He cannot change the features God gave him," her husband interrupted. "You know he is a highly gifted man and can do much good."

Kate maintained that he lacked stability and that he was overbearing. Only this morning he had called her "*Domina* Kate, ruler of heaven and earth." She had ignored this greeting, but this noon he had asked her, "And how is Juno, wife of Jupiter, who rules her husband?" When Kate took exception to this, he hurriedly attempted to modify it by telling her how Erasmus, whom he had met at a church celebration, had described Kate as very pretty. This flattery left her unmoved. She still felt that Agricola was a troublemaker and she was resentful when he dared disagree with her Doctor.

But Grikel was lovable. She was not as gay and lighthearted as Katy Jonas but she was even-tempered and helpful. Grikel was interested in the visiting Englishmen. Day after day she talked about the banquet which Kate was planning in their honor. Where would Kate get all the food? She had not long to wait. The weeks of preparation passed so quickly that Grikel was surprised when it was only a day off.

Kate called her downstairs one morning, "Look what Elector John Frederick just sent—a keg of wine and a wild boar. That'll mean hard work, my dear. The men are butchering a dozen chickens today. And Wolf is taking care of the fish. He also discovered some fine hare in the market."

"Oh!" Grikel stared, open-mouthed, "something for every taste. Kate, you are wonderful. But how will you manage with all these people?"

"Oh," Kate replied, "it's nothing. I've given many such big banquets and dinners. The children's baptisms were all like that. Then there were Doctor's birthdays and the graduations. Right now we're planning Lena Kaufman's wedding in about a year or so. Come now, Grikel, let's look over my linens." She started up the stairway into the big family room.

"But," Grikel said, following her, "Lena is only the Doctor's niece. You can't give weddings and outfits to all the orphaned nieces."

Kate shrugged. "We'll do it somehow. We are already planning Lena's dress. It will be very fine with gold embroidery and edging all around the neck. Doctor says that not even Solomon wore such finery. But as you know, she will marry Ambrose Brandt, professor of philosophy at the University. So everything must be the best."

Grikel gazed at her in admiration. "You and your Doctor," she commented, "you are a pair. You do so many good things. So much charity. And sometimes you get a bad deal in return, like that Rosina Truchsess. Didn't she steal?"

Kate hauled a pack of homespun linen cloths from the heavy chest. "Here," she said handing them to Grikel, "count these. We'll need about a dozen." Then she added solemnly, "As a rule Doctor and I don't discuss those things. He feels so deeply for all unfortunates. But since you already know—yes, things disappeared. Rosina acted so poor and pleaded so piteously when she came here that we couldn't turn her down. Soon the whole town began talking about her. They said she was immoral. When Doctor held this up to her, she broke down and begged forgiveness and promised to be good. Then, while he was away on a journey, she went back to her evil ways and I put her out of the house."

"And in spite of that you took in that widow who ran off with a rich Jew?"

"Yes, the poor woman was pregnant and he had been killed by a mob. She was so desperate from wandering about the country that we couldn't refuse her shelter. She had her baby here and Doctor baptized it. Afterwards, her brother became reconciled and took her home."

"And how about that poor Elizabeth of Denmark?"

"Oh, that's very sad. She took Communion according to Doctor's teaching, as the Bible states. Her little daughter told her father about it. He would have imprisoned her if she hadn't quickly fled. Now she is wandering all over the country, sick of body and heart and begging to come here. In fact, she may stand at the door any day."

"Tsk! Tsk! So much trouble," Grikel sighed. "And

so many poor people—young ones, old ones, widows, orphans, students, refugees—they all come here. How can you stand it?"

Kate smiled solemnly. "I don't know. God must give us the necessary strength. Sometimes I know that Doctor is completely exhausted and worn out. But look," she suddenly interrupted herself, "here comes Wolf to find out about the tables. Sit down a minute," she motioned to the gaunt man, who instantly obeyed her. Putting her hand to her chin and wrinkling her brow, Kate murmured, "Regularly, I have from twenty to thirty people. Now, I think, we can count on again as many. If all the professors come with their wives and the Englishmen and the Elector and a few other friends and notables . . . Can you get three or four tables ready?"

Wolf nodded his head. "I think so, Mrs. Luther. I'll get everything ready and set them up early tomorrow morning."

"Good Wolf!" Kate praised, drawing a deep breath. "And now to work, everybody. There's cleaning and dusting and polishing to be done. Flowers have to be picked and arranged. And there's all the cooking and baking to be done. Madge," she addressed the oldest, "you take charge up here and show the girls how to wait on the tables properly. Grikel and I will go downstairs and help the cooks and maids."

The kitchen was buzzing with activity. Smoke and smells were thick. In one corner the boar was being dressed for the revolving spit. The head would be roasted separately. There was mincing, chopping, and braying in mortars. Hannah was preparing meat jellies. Dorothy was busy with cheese. Chickens were soon ready for the iron pot with Grikel to watch over them. The hired cook was building a church of butter which was to be the centerpiece. Kate herself made the fruit dumplings and sweet cake, careful not to waste any of the precious loaf of sugar provided by Cranach. Flushed and perspiring, she worked late into the night. But she felt it was worth it.

The banquet the next day turned out entirely to her liking. The Englishmen relished her food and praised her beer. They liked the Elector's wine. They commented on Kate's thoughtfulness in arranging such a dinner in the midst of all the discussions, disputations, visitations, and meetings. All the professors had come with their wives. Even Philip Melanchthon's wife was there. Kate had seated Dr. Barnes at her right. Elector John Frederick sat at Luther's right. Kate and her Doctor had become deeply attached to Barnes. He had learned a little German during his various stays in Wittenberg. The learned bishop seated on her other side did not understand any German. Noticing this, Luther quipped, "I'll give you my wife for a teacher. She is very eloquent and far surpasses me." Barnes agreed that he already had found her so, as would the bishop also.

There was a great deal of bantering between them and much witty talk. Kate was happy to see her husband in excellent spirits. She couldn't help thinking of Anne and more than once was tempted to ask about King Henry and his new wife. But she could not do so without being overheard by those near. At the close of the meal, however, after they had sung and listened to singing by a selected choir, Barnes told her. They were about to leave the table when he turned back and whispered solemnly, "Word has just come to me that Anne has been executed, leaving a baby daughter."

Later, when Kate related this to her husband he said, "It's a monstrous thing. And Henry, as I thought, is impossible to deal with. He has no religion whatever." Kate could see how weary these weeks of strain had left her Doctor. He had also been deeply shocked at the sudden death of his good friend, Hans Mann. He had spells of weakness. But there would be more meetings to come and already he was talking of the great council meeting that was planned for February in Smalcald. This would be a most important gathering.

Kate tried to talk her husband out of going. He had been ailing since the Englishmen's banquet. As January neared its end his health improved. So, in spite of the cold and the snow, Luther insisted that he would go. Kate still disapproved. But when her husband's barber stepped into the house the day before departure and gave him a thorough grooming, she became reconciled to his going. Early on the following morning, which was the thirty-first of January, the Elector's carriage stopped at the Black Cloister for Luther. Kate and Madge went out to see him off and to greet Melanchthon, Bugenhagen, and Spalatin, already seated in the carriage and waiting. Kate begged her Doctor to take care of himself.

He kissed her and Madge fondly. "Remember," he said, a whimsical smile on his face, "Agricola is to take my place as housefather and have the children instructed every day. Weller is a faithful tutor. You, of course, are Master Kate, ruler of all."

That took the edge off the parting. They drove away, their wagon wheels grinding on the hard frozen ground, their breath making clouds in the cold air. Kate and Madge waved cheerfully, then ran in to look after the younger children. Since Hans had been packed off to school in Torgau, Madge shouldered his responsibility as well as her own toward the three younger children.

Kate had figured that the forty-five miles to Smalcald could not be made in less than six or seven days. In due time, Luther's letter came, saying that he had preached in Weimar the first Sunday. They had had a good trip and arrived in Smalcald on February 7. Here he had preached in the town church which was so big that his voice had sounded to him like a mouse's. He was enjoying the fresh air and thought he would stay four weeks. "My old enemy, the stone," he wrote, "bothers me some, due to the cold, damp Hessian beds, the medic says. However, the convention is slow in assembling. And I deplore the time lost and the too-good eating."

Kate breathed a sigh of relief and went about her work singing. Agricola came to her every day to confer with *Domina* Kate about the household. Sometimes she could tolerate his sweet, deferential manner when he called her "Juno" and "wife of Jupiter" and "Supreme Ruler." But at other times she coldly turned her back to him.

She had another letter soon saying that again her Doctor had preached before a large congregation and then had become violently ill. "I cannot now write all I would," he went on, "for I have been a useless man all day, owing to this painful stone and weakness. The doctors came and gave me physic as if I were a great ox. I was obliged to submit to horse cures of every kind."

After this, silence. Kate began to worry. She said to Grikel, "I am afraid I'll never see him again. Why did I let him go?"

Grikel tried to comfort her. Even Agricola ceased his quipping and spoke gently and seriously. Perhaps Master Philip had written his wife, he suggested. She might know something. Kate ran over to the Melanchthon home. Had Katherine heard from her husband? Had Philip written how Luther was? Yes, Katherine Melanchthon, hesitantly at first, admitted all. Philip had written how they had all expected him to die and how he, Philip, had wept like a woman. The Elector had stood at his bed, too, and promised to take care of his wife and children.

"But in all his pain," Katherine went on, "he tried to make them laugh. He said it was no art to drink *good* beer, but to drink *sour* beer. And he tried to comfort Philip by saying, 'If we receive good from the hand of God, shall we not also receive evil?' And . . ."

She could not go on for the tears that blurred her eyes, for even Katherine, who often so disgusted Kate with her standoffishness, deeply loved and honored Luther. Seeing this, strong Kate, too, broke down, and both women sobbed unrestrainedly. After a while Kate regained sufficient control of herself to ask, "And now—how is he now? Tell me, what are they saying about my Doctor now?"

Katherine could only shake her head and Kate suddenly bounded up. "I must go. I must go to him and nurse him. I must hurry home, Katherine. I'll order the horses hitched to the wagon and go at once. Goodbye."

She rushed home, calling as she entered the house, "Grikel, Aunt Lena, Madge, help me get ready! I must go to Smalcald . . ."

Before she could finish the sentence, a messenger with a note arrived from the Elector: "We have moved our beloved Doctor Martin from Smalcald because there the necessary medical instruments are not procurable. Dr. Sturtz is treating him. Bugenhagen and other friends are here with him. Today he is much better. So, I need not send the carriage for you after all."

The same messenger also had a note from her Doctor: "My beloved Kate—We are at Tambach. We could go only a few miles on the mountainous road. God worked a miracle: the jolting ride brought me relief. I now feel new-born. Thank God for me, dear Kate, and let the children also thank their heavenly Father. For I have been a dead man and commended you to God and our good Lord Jesus. I grieved very much for your sake, for I love you, my Kate, more than myself. You have been more than a wife to me. You have not been ashamed to serve me."

Kate gathered the entire household together at supper and had Agricola offer a prayer and asked the children to pray as well. Most touching of all was Madge's grief.

Her fervent prayer to the heavenly Father to bring her dear father back to them, alive and well, brought tears to all eyes.

Now going on eight years, the sweet, fine-featured child, with deep, expressive brown eyes like her father's, moved about the house in silence. Her sunny smile, so endearing to all who knew her, was overclouded. In her dark blue wool dress over a white bodice, which had a slightly starched collar and was laced at the front with a narrow ribbon, and her long brown hair hanging down over her neck, she was the picture of a charming, well-mannered child.

Madge confessed to her mother that she preferred to pray for her father when she was alone. Then she could talk more confidentially to God. Kate nodded, marveling that the child was so much like her father. She wished that Hans were home with them now, instead of in Torgau. Madge surprised her mother that night by coming to her bed, long after she was supposed to be asleep, and whispering, "Mother, I think God will let Father come home to us once more. So don't cry."

Kate quickly brushed her eyes with the back of her hand and said softly, "Yes, dear child."

A few days later, however, a messenger arrived with bad news. Dr. Luther was dying, he reported. He had had another relapse. But, the messenger said, the Doctor sent words of comfort to Kate, saying "how very much he loved her, how much she had done for him during the twelve years of their married life."

This time Kate stopped for nothing. Taking niece Lena

Kaufman with her, she set out at once, leaving the house to Aunt Lena and the Agricolas. On the way they were met by a messenger sent by the Elector to tell them that now the Doctor had passed the crisis of his illness and that he was entirely relieved of all his suffering. He would start for home soon and it was no longer necessary for Kate to come.

As if she would listen to that for one moment!

Kate and niece Lena went on. They found Luther resting at the home of a friend near Weimar. When they met and embraced, both burst into tears. And Lena joined them.

"Oh, how I longed for you," he said fervently, "when I was sick unto death! I thought I'd never see you and the children again. Now I love you more than ever, Kate. I would not trade you for all Venice and France."

Kate told him about Madge, how troubled she had been and how she had prayed for his recovery. She could see how deeply touched he was when he murmured, "The dear, sweet child." Then he asked, "And how is my big son, Hans, and the three little ones?"

Kate entertained him with family small talk, which he eagerly absorbed. Day after day she could see him improve. While he was still so weak that his legs barely carried him, she and Lena supported him between them. In a few days they could start the journey home. Here, gathered around the tile stove which Wolf kept well-fueled, recuperation made good progress.

"Father," Madge begged, one rainy March evening, as she snuggled close beside him, "could you tell us a story tonight? I remember the one about the dog that had a piece of meat and saw another dog with a piece of meat. Then he wanted that, too. And as he tried to snatch it he dropped the other and then he had nothing."

Martin and Paul, who had been playing on the floor, now pressed close to their father's knee.

"That was a stupid dog," Martin remarked.

"He was a greedy dog," Madge informed him, "and that's why he lost everything."

Kate looked up from her sewing to see her Doctor take little Margaret on his lap as he said lovingly, "Yes, Madge, that was right. That is the moral in the story. And some day I hope you can read all of Aesop's fables in your own language. He has written many more which I hope to translate and gather in a book, so that all little German boys and girls can read them."

Madge enthusiastically applauded and even Aunt Lena added a word of approval. "But," Kate thought, as she glanced anxiously in her direction, "Aunt Lena is not well. She never complains, yet there is something wrong. Of course, she's had a cold lately. But I must not let her do so much. Rather make that worthless Wolf do more. There he is sitting again in the far corner of the room, listening and watching everything."

She rose abruptly. "Doctor, I think Aunt Lena is very tired. Couldn't we have devotion so that she can go to bed?"

His eyes rested on the elderly woman a moment. "Yes, yes," he nodded. "Shall we sing as usual or are you too tired, Aunt Lena?"

"By all means," she responded warmly, "let the children sing. There is nothing I like better."

Madge suggested her favorite, "The Day is Past and Gone." After the singing, Luther said an evening prayer, then all joined in the Lord's Prayer and went to their rooms.

During the night Kate woke up suddenly. A feeling about Aunt Lena troubled her. Lighting a candle, she cautiously made her way to her aunt's room. She found her in a high fever. Not wishing to rouse the entire household, Kate did what she could to relieve her. She would stay at her bedside and, as soon as day dawned, she would send Wolf to get Dr. Schurf.

Aunt Lena grew worse. She became delirious. Her breathing grew labored. She mumbled something unintelligible. Toward morning she opened her eyes. "Kate," she whispered, "call Martin. Pray."

Kate rushed to her husband, who hurried to the sick woman's bedside. He took her feverish hand, and softly called her by name. "Aunt Lena, you are very ill?" When she nodded weakly, he said, "And you are ready to go to your heavenly home?"

She raised herself. "Yes, Martin, I know that my Redeemer lives."

Exhausted, she sank back. He took her hand, bent over her and said, "You will not die, but sleep away as in a cradle. And when the morning dawns, you will rise and live forever." Both he and Kate sank to their knees in silent prayer. Though they heard no last breath, both knew it was the end. When they arose from their prayer, Aunt Lena's soul had flown.

"A beautiful death," said Luther, taking his wife's hand and leading her to the big empty living-room where the new morning was just breaking. Kate wept. She saw her husband's genuine grief and Madge's tears. Hans came home for the funeral. The two younger boys lamented tearfully when told that Aunt Lena would not come back. Her gentle, helpful presence was missed by all. The entire household took her loss greatly to heart.

"Father," Madge asked in her artless way, "doesn't God love us any more, because he took Aunt Lena away?"

"God wanted to give our dear Aunt Lena rest," he explained. "She was old and very tired. God meant well with her."

"And we mustn't begrudge her that rest," Kate added. Then taking a note from her pocket and turning to Doctor, she handed it to him. "Here is a message from my brother Hans and his wife. They are coming for the funeral.

He glanced at it and merely nodded.

In spite of her sadness, Kate could not help smiling at the admiration with which the children regarded her brother. They were awed at this aristocratic Uncle von Bora and his fine wife. Uncle Hans wore a fur-trimmed cloak and a velvet hat with a big red feather. Around his neck he wore a fluted, white ruff on which his blond beard seemed to rest. The sleeves had cuffs to match. He also wore velvet pantaloons and ribbon garters at his knees. And at his side hung a sword. His wife, whom they were to call Aunt Eva, was resplendent with velvets and frills and feathers and laces, puffed sleeves, lockets and rings. She also seemed to awe the children, Kate thought.

There was much talk between them that Kate had to exclude the children from. Uncle Hans confessed to the Luthers that he was at the end of his funds. The old family estate at Zuelsdorf, into which his wife had put all her money, did not turn out as they had hoped. It was so dilapidated that it would require more money than he had at his disposal to get it back in good shape.

Kate was completely shocked when he suggested their buying it. "Even if we could buy it," she parried, turning to her husband, "how about that Boas garden we asked Chancellor Brueck about?"

"That deal is off," her Doctor replied. "I spoke with Brueck today and he has favored others. For some reason he doesn't seem to want us to have it."

"Oh," Kate sulked, "he doesn't like me. He has it in for me, that's all."

She caught Hans and his wife exchanging smiles and felt that she had acted rather childishly in their presence.

"Well," Hans suggested, "if you've had another deal that didn't materialize, all the more reason for you to consider this old family property. You have horses and a wagon, Kate. Why not drive out there tomorrow and look it over?"

Kate flushed with excitement, looked at her Doctor. Much to her surprise he consented. "Perhaps a ride through the country will do us all good after the strain and sorrow we've just had."

"But it's a long drive," Hans warned, "about two miles from Leipzig."

The two-day journey was interesting to Kate, in spite of the discomfort of riding in a clumsy vehicle over bumpy roads. She was, of course, flaming to buy this ancestral home then and there. But her Doctor said no, it was in such bad condition.

"In the first place," he said, "we can't afford it. Think, child, 610 gulden. Where will we get it?"

Kate was a bit tearful. "Well," she countered, "don't my boarders bring in something? Don't I supply all our own needs now? And do you know that I have three cows and nine calves? I will sell the calves. I have eight pigs, half of which I can sell. What of all the chickens, geese, ducks, and pigeons?"

Hans von Bora smiled sympathetically at his sister as her Doctor chucked her under the chin. "My dear Kate, even if we could buy it by some hook or crook, you would kill yourself to get it repaired and keep it so."

"Oh, but I'd love to try it."

"And look how far it is from home—two days coming and two days going."

"That can be done faster," she insisted doggedly. "And, anyway, it would be just a fine trip for the children and a wonderful place for you to rest up."

He shook his head. "My dear, bright Morning Star, you would never get any rest here. And, who knows, you might settle here for good and leave me," he concluded jestingly.

But Kate was not in a jesting mood. For once she felt frustrated. She bade her brother and sister-in-law, who were to go on to Leipzig, farewell and started home with her Doctor.

Little was said on the way. They had too much to think about. The coachman, who always drove when they went long distances, tried in vain to start a conversation.

It was growing dark when they entered the cloister grounds. Hardly had Kate alighted when Grikel stormed upon her. "Oh, Kate, thank God you're here at last."

"Why? Has something happened?"

"Yes," Grikel gasped excitedly, "she came . . . you know . . . the woman . . . Oh, that poor Elizabeth we talked about! And . . ." she sighed deeply, "we didn't know what to do with her. She just cries and cries."

"Oh, the poor dear soul!" At once Kate's warmhearted nature came to the fore. She pushed ahead of Grikel, sped up the circular stairway and peeped cautiously into the big living-room where, instead of dear old Aunt Lena, a distracted, red-eyed woman sat.

"Why, Princess Elizabeth!" Kate rushed up to her, caught her in a close embrace, kissed her, patted her arm, and murmured, "I am so glad you came, dear Princess. So glad you're here with us."

Elizabeth moaned softly and tried to repress her sobs. Suddenly she broke into an uncontrollable storm of tears. "Oh, Kate," she wailed brokenly, "thank God for you. I have . . . no one—no one . . . but you. They all hate me! My own daughter . . . tattled . . . because I had Communion . . . as Luther . . ."

She couldn't go on. Kate drew her down on a chair with her and stroked her arms. "I know, Princess," she soothed, "I know how you have been treated. I know how you have suffered. Try not to think of that now. Try to think how warm and cozy you're going to be here. And how I love you and will try to help you."

Elizabeth went into a fresh outburst. "Oh, Kate, please forgive me. I don't want to cry . . . and act like this. But, I can't help it. I have no strength."

"That's all right, Princess," Kate half sang these words, as if she were singing a baby to sleep. "Just let yourself go. Cry it out. By and by everything will get better."

And by and by the outbreaks lessened. The Princess quieted down. Kate wiped her damp face and said with a glint of a smile, "And now would you like to go to bed and sleep?"

Elizabeth sat bolt upright. "Oh," she said violently, "I can't sleep! I haven't slept for months."

Kate looked at her with all the love of a mother for her child. "But here you will sleep. Come, I'll show you the nicest, little room." She rose and took Elizabeth's hand, who followed her docilely.

In the room Elizabeth dropped into the nearest chair. "Oh, Kate," she sighed heavily, "I am so weak. I can't even lift . . ." again she gulped and threatened to break down.

"You needn't, dear Princess," Kate murmured in her softest voice, "you needn't do anything—just rest. I'll help you undress," she went on, beginning to unbutton and unhook her dress.

When she had helped her into a soft gown and loosened the heavy nut-brown hair, she adjusted the pillows and drew a warm cover over Elizabeth, who lay back completely exhausted.

"Now, Princess," Kate whispered in a mock serious voice, "don't you fall asleep until I get back. I'm going to bring a nice, warm drink," she smiled encouragingly, "and I know you'll sleep like a baby."

Elizabeth's eyes filled with tears. "Oh, Kate, you are an angel. God bless you."

Hours later, when Kate peeped into the room, her patient was sleeping peacefully.

"Poor dear," Kate said to Doctor when she related the evening's experience to him, "she has completely broken down, physically and spiritually. What she needs is rest and more rest, good food, peace of mind and much, much love."

"Can you love her enough?" he asked.

"No, Doctor. We must all show her love and consideration."

"And above all," he added seriously, "we must always keep her in mind of God's great love. That will be the most healing of all."

Kate sighed. "I'm afraid it's going to take a long, long time to nurse her back to health. She is so utterly broken."

"With God's help nothing is impossible," he encouraged her. "So don't be afraid."

Chapter 14

Life was like a seesaw, Kate thought that early spring morning as she sat in her Doctor's study watching the Elbe. She was just recovering from a severe illness and, as she leaned back in the pillows he had arranged for her in his own great chair, she smiled faintly.

In stormy waves the river swept by. One moment the sun was there, its glittering rays carried along on the crest of the waves; the next moment the rays disappeared and a dark, forbidding stream rolled by. Wasn't life just like that: stormy rain followed by bright sunshine—tears by laughter?

In spite of everything, it was good to be alive. The past three years had been unusually difficult. Since Peter had gone to the Holy Land, they had heard from him only once. Kate was convinced that they would never see him again. Aunt Lena's death the same year had cut deeply. The entire household had missed her gentle helpfulness during the many sicknesses there had been. And —Kate covered her mouth and sighed unrestrainedly— the most trying of all had been nursing the unhappy

Elizabeth of Denmark. It had taken seven months of the most tender care to get the Princess back on her feet. Her daughter had finally come and taken her home. After that there had been various sicknesses among students, boarders, children, and servants. Worst of all was another visit by the dreaded plague. Naturally, the university students and most of the professors hurried away. One of the professors lost his wife and was, himself, so seriously ill that Kate had taken pity on him and his family and nursed them in her own home. In some parts of Wittenberg the plague had attacked with such violence that whole families fled the city. Infested houses were torn down and burned. Again the Elector had implored Luther to flee and again he had refused to be intimidated. He visited the sick and the dying and begged grain and food from the Elector for the living.

Kate realized now what a great toll these past three years had exacted from her. Her own foot trouble and her Doctor's frequent indisposition, and the strain of all the other burdens had finally overcome her in January. Sick unto death she prayed Psalm 31 which she had memorized:

> In thee, O Lord, do I seek refuge; let me never be put to shame; in thy righteousness deliver me! . . . Into thy hand I commit my spirit, thou hast redeemed me, O Lord, faithful God . . . Be gracious to me, O Lord, for I am in distress, my eye is wasted from grief, my soul and my body also . . . But I trust in thee, O Lord, I say, "Thou art my God." My times are in thy hand . . . O how abundant is thy

goodness which thou hast laid up for them who fear thee . . . Be strong and let your heart take courage, all you who wait for the Lord!

Over and over she had repeated the whole psalm, while she still had strength and consciousness. When she finished she had heard Master Philip's faraway, soft voice, "She has strong faith, Martinus."

As in a dream she had heard her Doctor's reply: "Is it not always so? When women accept the teaching of the gospel, they are much stronger and more fervent in faith. They hold to it more firmly than men. Mary Magdalene was braver than Peter."

Kate had heard it and forgotten. Strange that now suddenly she should remember it. She could see her husband hover over her. Day and night he was at her side. She had a vague memory of him and the children down on their knees praying for her recovery. How far away their voices had sounded. Then she had lost consciousness. But God heard her family's prayer and answered it. She came up from the depths.

After a few days she could feel life flooding back in her veins. Then she knew she would recover. Dr. Schurf told her so, but warned that recovery would be slow. And so it was. She had to be held by her husband the first few times after leaving her bed. After that she held on to chairs, tables, and doors. How she longed for Aunt Lena then, or Elsie, or gay little Katy Jonas. But the Jonases had left Wittenberg and moved to Halle. And Grikel—the good, helpful soul—had left the city and moved to Berlin with her family. Kate did not like to think of it all. She and Grikel were still good friends, but the men had had a falling out and the Doctor had severed the ties of friendship between them because Agricola had undertaken to teach and preach what Luther could never accept. He had forgiven Agricola, but the old friendship could never be the same. Kate was free to associate with Grikel and invite her to the house, but that was all.

This still troubled Kate. Household affairs also troubled her. Since there was no Aunt Lena, no Grikel, no niece Lena Kaufman to take charge of the brewing during her illness, there hadn't been any beer in the house for months. No beer soup for breakfast. Just barley gruel. Poor old Hannah and Dorothy had too much to do as it was. The younger nieces, even Anna Straus, who was looking for a suitable husband, could not be trusted with it. Kate was also worried about refusing to board a few young people because there was no more room in the house. But to offset this, there had been that messenger from Nuremberg, bringing a precious goblet which had been willed to them by the father of one of their former students.

She was thinking of this, and smiling, when she heard her Doctor's footsteps. He burst into the room like a happy boy. When he swept his hat off his head and bowed low before her, she broke into laughter.

"Doctor, what does this mean?"

He took her hand and kissed it. "My new Queen, my most gracious Lady of Zuelsdorf—the estate is yours."

"Oh, Doctor! Dear Doctor!"

He sat down beside her and, taking her hand between

his own, said soberly, "Yes, Kate, your wish is at last fulfilled. The good Elector, as usual, has helped out. He gave Hans von Bora six hundred gulden and me the deed. He promised to furnish the lumber for repairs. That will run high because the place is, as you know, badly neglected."

Kate was so overwhelmed she could not find words. Her childhood home! The home in which she had never really lived. A hundred thoughts swarmed into her head. Already she could see herself and the Doctor there, spending their last days in peace and quiet—away from Wittenberg and all its turmoil. So lost in thought was she that she started violently at his voice close beside her, "Kate, have you nothing to say? Are you not pleased?"

Then she bounded up and, throwing her arms around his neck, half sobbed, "Forgive me, dearest Doctor. Yes, I am happy, very happy. I have no words to thank you." And, after a while, she asked shyly, "When can I go there?"

"It's still cold," he said thoughtfully, "and the spring air is sharp. You'd better wait a little. May will soon be here with warm days. Then my Lady of Zuelsdorf shall ride out to her new estate."

His manner was so boyishly gay that they both laughed. Just then the door opened and Madge hurried in. She held little Margaret before her.

"Father! Mother!" she was breathless with excitement. "I heard you laugh. I couldn't wait. May I come in?" When her father nodded, she shoved Margaret ahead of her.

"Come here, my darling," Kate called yearningly. Then,

as the five-year-old, chubby little girl snuggled close, she said, "I don't get to see my children at all any more. What have you been doing all day?"

"Oh," Madge explained in her sweet, grave way, "this morning we studied our catechism and Bible history and the Psalms. Margaret is learning a verse that she'll say on my birthday."

"Your birthday?" her father exclaimed. "Yes," he added, "that is right. In a few days it will be May 4, and then you'll be eleven years old."

"Yes, Father. I'm growing up now."

Kate remarked, "You're really getting big. Soon this dress will not fit you any more. But now tell me about Martin and Paul. Were they good boys?"

Madge nodded. "A little tricky sometimes. They watched Wolf make nets . . ."

"Nets?" The Doctor rose to his feet. "That miserable Wolf! Is he at it again? Haven't I strictly forbidden him to snare birds?" He started for the door. "Kate, I must go. I cannot permit such practices."

Madge clung to his arm. "Oh, Father, maybe I should not have told you."

"Indeed you should. Too often things are not told a father. And that should not be."

Kate watched them go out. She hoped nothing would happen. Such things could make the Doctor very angry, and he would not hesitate to punish Martin and Paul severely, just as he had punished Hans.

She did not see him again until at the supper table, when he seemed depressed and lost in thought. Wolf was subdued and the two boys were shy. The meal passed without the usual conversation. The next morning he did not appear at the breakfast table. Nor at dinner. When he did not come for supper, Kate became uneasy. No one had seen Doctor Luther. They had missed him at lectures. Even Melanchthon had not seen him. The second day passed without a trace of him. Kate tried the door of his study and found it locked. But he couldn't be inside because there was no response. Where could he be? Could he have fallen into the Elbe one of these windy spring nights? Could he have gone to the woods and lost his way? Finally, the third morning Wolf came in with a letter he had found hung on a tree. The letter was from the birds, accusing Wolf and begging him not to snare them. Then the truth dawned upon Kate. She sent Wolf out to get a locksmith. She would open the door to the Doctor's study by force. When the door at last was opened, they beheld a tired, surprised-looking man sitting among papers and books.

"Doctor!" Kate's voice had a certain hurt ring, "why did you do this?"

He faced her calmly. "Did you think that I was up to some mischief here?" He shook his head. "I was in need of solitude to get some work done. I'm up to my ears in work—tracts to write, letters and sermons to write—and the house so noisy."

"But what did you eat? I hope you didn't fast these three days?"

He pointed to a plate with a remnant of herring on it.

"A crust of bread, a bit of herring, a mug of water was all I needed. It gave me a clear head for thinking."

Kate said resolutely, "Come, my dear Doctor, no more of this. Tomorrow is Madge's birthday and we must celebrate. And look what a warm day it is. Come outside with me," she said, smiling at him, "and let's take a look at our pear tree."

When he still hesitated and looked with anxious eyes at the maze of books and sheets strewn about, she begged lovingly, "Please! Just a few minutes. The air will be good for you." She gently pulled him after her.

"As usual," he groaned in comic despair, "Master Kate has her way."

The pear tree was just beginning to bloom. They sat down on the stone bench, inhaling the fragrant May air and listening with amusement to the barnyard noises. Soon he rose and turned to go. "I really feel refreshed now, Kate," he said cheerfully. "If I catch up with all my work and the weather is good, we'll drive out to Zuelsdorf on Pentecost after the service."

Kate was exuberant. She was beginning to feel stronger every day. She told the children about Zuelsdorf and how the von Boras had lived there for about three hundred years, so that they were all excited. They went to the early Pentecost service that Sunday and, after a hurried lunch, piled into the high-seated, wooden-wheeled wagon. Kate saw to it that a supply of covers and bedding was taken along. The servants had packed a large basket of food. When all were comfortably seated the coachman cracked his whip and they were off. They stopped for the night at Torgau and lodged with Hans's schoolmaster. Kate told Madge how she and the other nuns had been carted here from the convent that Easter morning about seventeen years before. Madge was interested. She had often heard bits of the story. Now she was able to visualize it more clearly.

Early the following morning they started out again, taking Hans with them. The May morning was brilliant. Fields and orchards everywhere glistened with freshness and with white blossoms. The air was sweet with spring odors. Birds warbled and sang. Farmhouses, clustering close together, formed picturesque little villages along the way. Everywhere men, women, and children were busy in the fields.

"Look, children," Kate exclaimed, pointing into the distance, "over there—do you see that steeple peeping out—that's the church at Nimbschen on the convent grounds. A little farther is Grimma."

"Is the convent empty now?" Leni wondered.

"Yes, the sisters have all left. Even the abbess finally went."

"What are they doing with all the buildings?" Hans asked.

"That depends," his father said. "Sometimes the church claims them; sometimes the state."

Kate's eyes rested on her first-born with all the old affection. How fast he was growing up. At fourteen, he was as tall as his father. Slender, good-looking, and so well-behaved, Kate thought, that even her Doctor was happy with him. Evidently his years of school and training in Torgau were not lost.

"Do you see those mountains in the far distance?" asked Luther. "They belong to the Ore Mountains."

Madge shuddered. "Oh, Father, I read some stories about the terrible giants who live there!"

"Just tales!" Hans berated. "There are no giants."

Madge, as usual, turned to her father. "Is that true, Father? Are there no giants? Then how about Goliath?"

His eyes had a faraway look. "We don't know what's in those mountains," he said. "There are many, many things about this earth of ours that we don't know—as yet. But the Bible tells us that 'there were giants in those days.' "

Madge couldn't resist a smile of triumph.

"See, Hans," she nodded, "there are, all right."

His frown of boyish annoyance suddenly changed to an expression of delight. "Leipzig," he said, "that's the big, wonderful city of Leipzig we're coming to. Will we stop there?"

"No," Kate said, "we haven't time. It's out of our way. When you're older you can go there. Now we have about two or three more miles to Zuelsdorf."

Some time later, Luther shifted his position. "This slow driving," he said, "makes you feel stiff. But," he added cheerfully, "we'll soon be there, Kate. Only don't feel too discouraged."

She laughed gaily. "Discouraged? Dear Doctor, how you talk! The place is run-down. But I can repair it to look like new. That's just what I love to do. I'll make a nice, cozy home of it—a place of refuge for us when we're old. Look, we're getting there!"

In her excitement, she stood up in the wagon. Her eyes glowed. "Children," she cried, "look! There it is—Zuelsdorf—your mother's ancestral home. Here is where the von Boras lived since the thirteenth century."

The children craned their necks. The Doctor looked. Kate looked at the group of weather-beaten buildings as if with one magic word she could replace them with a beautiful palace and handsome stables. Martin plainly showed his disappointment. "Is that your home? It looks like all the buildings are falling apart."

"Which one were you born in?" Paul asked. "They must be old!"

Kate was undismayed. "I'm only forty-three, Paul. That isn't old. And I lived there only till I was five. Then my mother died and my father took me to an orphanage."

Madge looked thoughtful. "I don't think it's so bad here. After you get it all fixed up, it'll be a grand place for us."

Kate nodded appreciatively. "Of course."

"Well, Mother," Hans put in sagely, "after it's all shipshape, we'll have a home all our own."

The coachman drove through the high grass and weeds as close to the entry as he could, then stopped the horses, looked at them over his shoulder and said, "This is Zuelsdorf, Doctor Luther."

Kate's eyes swept the forsaken grounds.

"What a wilderness," her Doctor remarked as they plucked their way through weeds and quack grass to the nearest house door which had a rusty lock and hinges. Once an imposing building, it was actually crumbling to pieces.

Kate touched one of the loose windowpanes, remarking, "All it needs is repair. Remember the Black Cloister grounds! These buildings and gardens are not any worse than those were when I came there. And," she added triumphantly, surveying it all, "it's ours to do with as we please. Zuelsdorf is ours!"

Chapter 15

Spring became summer. But no matter how early the sun rose, the "Morning Star of Wittenberg" rose still earlier. Kate was her old vigorous self again. With Zuelsdorf on her hands, she was busier than ever, directing building and repairing. Zuelsdorf—home of her ancestors! Zuelsdorf—home of her old age!

Just as Kate had transformed the gloomy Black Cloister into a friendly, hospitable home, so she was now converting von Bora ruins into a paradise. Just as she had made all her gardens produce, so now within a year Zuelsdorf began to produce. Some of her prolific barnyard populace was transferred to Zuelsdorf. She could easily subtract a pair from each of the species and still leave enough at home. This year she counted five cows and nine calves, ten pigs and half a dozen piglets, one goat and three kids, and four horses. She had already sold so many young pigs that her Doctor addressed her as "Lady of the Pig Market." Because she spent so much of her time at Zuelsdorf during this first year, he wrote to her often.

"My most gracious Lady of Bora and Zuelsdorf, the

wealthy, honored Katherine Luther, who bodily lives in Wittenberg but in her heart is ever in Zuelsdorf," he would write. Kate knew, whenever she received one of these letters that her Doctor was lonely. But Hannah and Dorothy were there to manage the household. Kate could not rest until Zuelsdorf was habitable and its garden and orchard cared for. Her indomitable will swept aside all interference.

Great was the rejoicing when Kate came home to stay a while. Then the old Black Cloister became the home incomparable. These summer evenings she loved to sit under the pear tree with her Doctor, watching him frolic with the children or listening to the stories he told them. They were both droll and serious. Though he had so little time for pleasure and only grudgingly made social calls, he was always interested in everything the children did.

When little Margaret handed him a rose she had just picked, he looked at it a long time, turning it this way and that way. Then he said, "If a person could make one single rose like this, then he should be given a kingdom. Notice the beautiful color and the perfume! We take all this for granted because we're so used to it. But if God should one day withhold fresh air and sunshine, what would become of us? If we could get rid of sin and death, we would never look for a better paradise."

Yes, it was paradise, Kate thought. This was the best year since Aunt Lena had died. For once there was no sickness to speak of. The children were well, her Doctor was in good health and spirits, she herself was well again, and everything had been coming out all right. Again and again she realized the truth of Luther's statement in praise of marriage and family life.

Sitting at the table, her husband on one side, her children on the other, Kate enjoyed every minute of the varied conversation. Among the newcomers there was John Mathesius, who had confided to Kate that to be a guest at Dr. Luther's table he considered the greatest honor of his life. He took down notes with the utmost care, for he planned to collect them in a volume entitled *Table Talk.* He also hoped to write the story of Doctor Luther's life.

On this particular day in late June, as the Doctor looked up from his plate at the company seated around his dinner table, he broke out jovially, "Well, you prelates, has anything new happened anywhere? Who knows something of interest?" Kate held her breath and glanced at Mathesius. He was watching one of the young students who seemed to be bursting to speak. He was kept down, however, by those next to him, who asked the Doctor to begin by relating some experience. He agreed, his eyes atwinkle.

"There was once a man here with his son to ask my advice about a profession for the boy. He was long-winded and hard to shake and trying his best to convince me that his son was brilliant. Meanwhile, the lout of a boy kept moving about the room, examining everything. He was still talking when dinner-time came around and the servants set in the middle of the table a roasted goose with a crisp brown crust. The man was too intent talking to me to notice his hopeful offspring move to the table, pick up a knife, cut into the goose, and pull off a long strip of the crisp skin. He did this again and then again. When he was about to start for the fourth time, I jumped up and said to the stunned father, 'Your son should be a tanner. You see how cleverly he has already half-skinned this goose.' "

Laughter and murmured applause followed. Next, a serious-faced student wanted to know about Solomon. How was it that he could have so many wives? Kate was all ears. It was gratifying to hear her Doctor's reply.

"Very likely," he explained, "there were many poor, neglected girls from David's court and among his relatives who had no other place to stay."

"Could this custom of plural wives ever be revived?"

"It's not likely," Luther said. "The women would not permit it."

Kate bounded up, blushing furiously. "If they ever did," she burst out vehemently, "I'd run away and never come back." She sat down, resting her head in her hand and her elbow on the table.

Another student asked, "If Eve brought us all to damnation, then why did not Christ bring salvation to all?"

Kate glanced at her Doctor as he replied, "Did not God give his Son for all? Then, plainly, He brought salvation to all."

The young student who had been bursting to talk could be held back no longer. Red-faced he rose and asked boldly, "Doctor, what was God doing before He created the world?"

Kate held her breath, as everyone seemed to be doing. She saw Madge wince as she always did when she thought her father might be displeased. Promptly the answer came in scathing words, "At that time God was sitting in the woods whittling birch switches for young whippersnappers like you."

That punctuated the meal. Luther gave the signal to rise. He spoke the blessing and had the children speak theirs. Kate tried to relieve the momentary embarrassment by suggesting a game of bowling. Half of the company moved away in the direction of Wolf's bowling alley. Madge, of course, walked beside her father. Martin and Paul hurried ahead to set up the pins. Kate arrived a little later, just as a great shout went up among the bowlers.

"Who's the champion?" she asked curiously.

"Oh," her Doctor laughed triumphantly, "I'm ahead of Philip."

Merriment was great among the students. The young fellows had a way, Kate observed with amusement, of swinging the ball and bringing the pins down at a lick. Philip Melanchthon was at it. He balanced the ball, swung it awkwardly and missed all but one pin. Laughter followed. Now her Doctor picked up the heaviest ball. But he swung it so awkwardly that it ran entirely off the alley. When they laughed at him, he joined in heartily.

"You young fellows," he said gayly, "you think we old fellows can't do anything. But wait till you get where we are," shaking his finger at them. "Look, Kate," turning to his wife, "over at the other end they are practicing fencing. That's good sport, too."

"Some of them are crossbow shooting. So long as they don't hurt my animals, I have no objection."

"Let them enjoy good, wholesome sport," he said, turning to go. "I must get back to work. And it's time for the children to get back to school, too."

Madge caught up with him and took his hand, Kate followed with Melanchthon, Margaret, and the two boys.

"Look," Luther said, addressing the boys, "Phil and Justy are already waiting. The tutor will lose patience if you don't hurry. Soon, my Madge, you won't need to go with the little ones any more."

She looked up into his face with her sunny smile. "But I don't mind, Father. One has to learn the catechism over and over, else one forgets it."

"Yes, dear child," he nodded, "just learn it well. And now other boys and girls, too, all over the country are going to learn about God and about praying to Him."

Kate always felt deeply touched at the love between the father and daughter. She loved them all loyally but realized that she had an especially soft spot for big Hans. Maybe he was not an angel. He had been naughtier than the other children, excepting Paul who always seemed so ready to fight that the Doctor called him a militarist. But Paul did not receive the rigorous training and the criticism that poor Hans had to take, and Hans had had to leave home so early. But this tender spot for her eldest did not diminish Kate's love for the younger ones.

She was looking forward right now to another trip to Zuelsdorf. The men working in the fields and repairing the buildings needed watching. She would be back in a few days. Later, in the fall, during harvesttime she would go again. Perhaps her Doctor would go with her then, for he was interested in this Zuelsdorf which she was "transforming from a sandy waste to a fruitful garden spot." But Luther was too busy to spend his time visiting and driving about the country. He complained that he had enough work to keep several secretaries busy. Kate, herself, was so occupied with her gardens and new estate that she didn't know where time stood. She hardly missed Grikel now, or Katy Jonas who had moved to Halle.

Before she realized it, Christmas was upon them. During the recitation of the glorious story of the nativity and the singing of the Christmas hymns, it seemed to Kate that Madge's voice was stronger and sweeter than it had ever been. The child would be twelve this coming May and was turning into young womanhood. Hans' voice was changing. But Martin and Paul sang lustily, and seven-year-old Margaret joined in with all her heart. Old Wolf settled behind the tile stove, as usual, munching nuts and sweets.

In January, 1545, Luther had a badly infected ear. Kate tried her best to combat the infection with hot applications. The Elector sent his own physician, but even he brought no relief. Kate could see the pain in her Doctor's eyes and in his contracted features. The inflammation deprived him of his hearing. He neither ate nor slept. Madge hovered about her father as much as Kate herself did. Finally, one cold morning the infected area opened from the outside. This brought immediate relief.

As the weeks went on the Doctor improved. Kate's

quick eye, however, detected something about him that made her question him one evening when they were alone. "Doctor, are you feeling better?"

"Why, yes."

"You have seemed so quiet lately. You walk about in deep thought, then stop and look at me as if you had something to tell me."

"I have—but it is very sad—and I hesitated to tell you."

His eyes dimmed. She waited patiently.

"It's about Barnes—our good English friend."

He paused again, swallowed painfully, then burst out vehemently, "Barnes is a saint now. Henry had him burned to death!"

An anguished scream escaped Kate. "Oh, what a monster that Henry is—may God have mercy on his soul. But, Doctor," she went on, after a while, "grieving won't bring Barnes back. You always . . ."

"Yes, yes, Kate, I know I always tell you to trust in God. I do, but still one has thoughts. And Barnes' death reminds me so strongly of how uncertain life is. Haven't I told you that many a time?" He bounded up from his chair, walked across the room, returned to his chair and drew it up opposite her. "Kate," he said, taking her hands, "what has happened to Barnes could happen to me."

"Oh, no!" she shuddered, withdrawing her hands and covering her eyes.

He took both hands and held them in his warm clasp. "Remember, Kate, you are my beloved, legal wife. I love you more than I love myself. You have been everything to me—mother, sister, wife, companion, housekeeper, nurse, bearer of my children, and a hundred more things. Now . . ." She sensed the depth of his feeling by the way his hands clasped and unclasped. His voice became a bit uncertain. "Kate," he asked suddenly, "what would you do if God called me away and you were left alone with the children?"

She started violently. "Dear Doctor," she cried, "not yet. Not yet. Just when life is sweetest. Besides, you are far from old. And God needs you."

He put his hand ever her mouth. "God needs no one to do His work. He can achieve all things without us poor mortals."

"But," she faltered, tears coming to her eyes.

"Kate," he said gently, "I did not mean to frighten you. But God wants us to think of these things and to put our house in order. So that is what I have done."

She sat back weakly, gazing at him. "Do you mean . . . you made your will?"

He nodded solemnly, "Yes, I've made my will. You know, perhaps, that the world is very cruel to widows. If I were to go suddenly, they would take away from you the little you have and give it to the children. And I feel that you should not be dependent on the children, but the children on you. Therefore, my dear, faithful, beloved wife, you are to have everything there is—Zuelsdorf, the little house we bought here in Wittenberg, the gardens, household goods, money, silver mugs and jewelry, and whatever else there is. God knows it is little enough."

Kate could keep back her tears no longer. "Oh, dearest

Doctor, you have always been a kind and considerate husband, thank you!"

He caught her arm and helped her out of the chair. "Come," he said, going to the window and opening it for a moment, "take a look outside at the clear, cold winter night. The snow crackles underfoot and sparkles in the moonlight."

Kate could not forget this evening's conversation. It haunted her for weeks afterward. She was glad when Katy Jonas wrote in April, announcing her prospective visit in June.

"Then I'll take her and the children out to Zuelsdorf for a week or two," Kate told her Doctor. "It'll be much prettier than it was last year."

He had no objection to her plans, especially since Katy was bringing her daughter Madeline to keep Madge company. When they arrived in Zuelsdorf, nature was at its best. The weather was glorious. Vegetation was luxuriant. Kate and Kathy roamed about the place with their daughters. Over and over Katy Jonas exclaimed, "This is heavenly, heavenly." When they returned in July, Kate dropped the Jonases off at Leipzig, from where they went home to Halle. She entertained a few other old friends, among them Elsie von Kanitz, with whom she talked over old times. Elsie told her that both Schoenfeld sisters had married well. Loneta had married twice, her first husband having been killed. The Staupitz sisters, who had been teaching for many years, were now both married. She knew nothing about the others.

After a month at home, Kate had to go back to Zuelsdorf to supervise work. Letters from her Doctor soon followed. She read through the lines that he was lonely. Again she saw his old worry that she was trying to make her heaven on earth and forgetting the real heaven. He begged her to sell her produce and come home soon. Please!

Kate could not stay after that. She gave instructions to her workers, packed, and hurriedly left. She had been in Zuelsdorf only two weeks. In Wittenberg, grapes, pears, peaches, and apples were beginning to need attention. Already the days were growing shorter. Wolf was getting the tile stove ready for the winter. With so much awaiting her here, with husband, children, students, and visitors all depending on her, Kate was glad to be home. The summer, she thought, was over too soon. September came and Hans departed for Torgau once again. The rainy season set in. It was cozy then to sit with the family in the big living-room on those rare occasions when her Doctor could spend a little time with them.

Kate didn't worry much when Madge went to bed feeling ill one evening. Children often ailed slightly. But next morning Kate was seriously alarmed.

"Doctor," she whispered to her husband, "our Madge is sick—terribly sick."

He had just come from the child's room. "I fear the worst," he nodded brokenheartedly.

"I think she knows it herself."

"Do you think Hans should come home?"

"Without delay. That was the first thing Madge asked me this morning. We should call Schurf, too."

"I'll call him and send Wolf to Torgau to get Hans," the Doctor said, moving toward the door.

"It might help her to get better," Kate added hopefully. Then, slowly, she entered the sick room on tiptoe.

Madge turned her feverish face and looked at Kate with burning eyes. "Hans," she murmured, "is Hans coming?"

"Yes, my darling," her father said, coming in just then, "Hans will come just as soon as he can." He brushed his sleeve across his eyes and stepped up to the bed. Madge's eyes were again closed. Her breathing was rapid. Kate stood beside her husband and put her hand in his for comfort.

The door opened softly and Dr. Schurf came in. He examined her and shook his head. "Mysterious," he whispered guardedly, "I can't diagnose it, but it's serious. Madge," he asked, when the child presently opened her eyes, "how do you feel? Have you any pain?"

Madge smiled faintly. "Nothing hurts me," she said. "I'm only hot."

Kate went out of the room with the puzzled physician. She went to the kitchen to see what Hannah and Dorothy were doing. It was nearing dinner time. When Martin, Paul, and Margaret came in from school, she hushed them.

"You must be quiet," she told them. "Your sister is very ill."

"Can't we see Madge?" they begged in unison.

She led them into the room, and they looked at their father, sitting in a chair beside the bed, his head buried in his hands. Kate knew he was weeping. No wonder—his darling! His Madge! His so dearly beloved child!

Oh, God, she thought, will you tempt him as you tempted Abraham or will you really take her away from him? It will kill him. Oh, God, have mercy on us! Let us keep her.

She stood there, while Margaret and her brothers gazed uncomfortably at their sister, not knowing how to act. Kate whispered, "Go, have your dinner and be good and pray for Madge." She put her hand on her husband's arm. "Doctor, it's dinner time," she said. "I'll stay here with her while you have a bite to eat."

"Eat?" he shook his head sadly. Then he rose. "But I will go out for a breath of air."

It seemed like a long time before he returned, bringing Schurf with him. Again the physician looked puzzled, and shook his head solemnly. "I'm sorry," he said, "I can hold out no hope. I know of no remedy for this sickness —it is most unusual." With this he backed out of the room.

Kate sighed and looked at her Doctor. "The afternoon drags and drags along," he complained. "When will our Hans come?"

She went to the nearest window, then to another, then to all the other windows. Oh, Hans, come quickly! Oh, Wolf, hurry, hurry, bring him home in time! Nothing could be seen or heard. Slowly, she returned to her husband. He was sitting beside the bed as before, watching his motionless child.

"They can't get here until evening," she remarked, "no matter how fast Wolf drives." Stepping to the bed, she leaned over to look at Madge long and carefully, then shook her head sorrowfully. "So ill, so ill," she moaned softly, "and no one to help her and no Hans here yet! My poor child!"

She sat down beside her Doctor, silently counting the time. One hour. Three hours. Endless hours dragging by. And the child lying there in a fever that could not be broken. Oh, Hans, when are you coming? She was startled out of her revery when the door opened and Martin called excitedly, "Mother, they're coming!"

The horses were galloping into the yard. She heard them before she could run out. "Oh, Hans," she caught her eldest in her arms.

"Mother, what is it?" he begged frantically. "We galloped all the way to get here, but Wolf wouldn't tell me."

He started to race into the house ahead of her. She held him back. "No, Hans. Calm yourself first. One can't go into a sick room like that. And Madge . . ."

"Then it *is* Madge," Hans sobbed.

Kate took his arm, helped him remove his cloak and cap, and said, "Brush your hair back and wash your hands and take a deep breath. Our Madge is very ill but you must not cry. You must be strong."

She led the way, pausing at the threshold to look at her Doctor, who was still sitting in the same position. When Kate called him, he looked up startled, his deep, brown eyes dimmed by tears. "Hans, my boy," he said, arising and embracing his son, "thank God you're here."

At the mention of her brother's name, Madge's eyes opened. She smiled and held out her hand, an expression of love in her face. She tried to raise her head but sank back exhausted.

"Hans," she whispered, "dear brother."

He bent down and kissed her. Kate withdrew to the farthest end of the room, her body shaking convulsively. Her husband, with bowed head and hands clasped behind his back, walked slowly away. Hans sat down on the edge of the bed whispering to his sister. Kate feared this might increase her fever, yet she could not summon courage to call the boy away. At last she spoke to him, telling him to sit in a chair while she and his father went to look after things. They would take turns watching, she said, and Hans could be first. Kate's turn came after midnight. Fatigued with the worries of the day and night, she dozed off. When she awoke, morning was dawning and Madge seemed to be resting quietly. Kate breathed lighter. The child must be getting better. A little later, when Melanchthon came to inquire, Kate related the dream she had had during the night.

"I saw them come into the room," she said, "two young men dressed in shining white. They said they were taking Madge to a wedding. And now," she added hopefully, "I think she must be getting well."

Melanchthon shook his head and looked serious. "These beautifully dressed young men," he explained, "are angels. They will come and lead your dear daughter to the heavenly marriage."

Kate knew it was true. When she met her husband coming into the room, she could see that he, too, knew. He nodded at Philip, who left the room.

"Dear God," she heard him murmur fervently, his hands tightly clasped, "I love her so much, but—" his voice broke and for a while he could not go on, then he caught himself, "but Thy will be done. I will be glad to know that she is with Thee, dear Saviour."

Hans came in quietly. The three younger children followed but, awed and bewildered, kept their distance. Kate sobbed quietly. She clung to her husband. She could feel him tremble. He bent down to the child and called gently, "Madge." She opened her wide eyes. A faint smile hovered on her feverish face.

"Little Madge," he said again, "dear daughter, you would gladly stay here with your father? And . . ." he paused to regain his natural voice, "you would also gladly go to your heavenly Father?"

With a look full of love and trust she said, "Yes, dear Father. As God wills."

It was too much for Kate. She tore herself from her husband's arms and went to the farthest corner of the room, covering her face with her apron. She heard her husband say, "You dear child . . ." then he too broke down. She felt his arms around her, trying to brace her, as he consoled her, "Kate, dear, remember how she is going. She is going to be in Paradise now with our dear Saviour."

Once more they dried their tears and prayed for strength as they stepped again to the bed, where Hans stood grieving. Madge's eyes now were wide open as if fixed on some distant object. As in a dream Kate saw her husband go down on his knees, holding the child in his arms while she drew her last breath. Then he gently placed her down, closed her eyes, pulled the sheet over her and said, "Darling Madge, how well off you are. You will rise again and shine as a star. Yes, as the sun. It is a wonderful thing," turning to his weeping Kate and Hans, "to know she is surely at peace, and yet at the same time—to be so sorrowful. We Christians are not to mourn. We know that it must be so, for we are sure of eternal life."

He led them out of the room, all three now weeping unrestrainedly. In the living-room they met Melanchthon. He wept with them. When the first storm of grief had passed, the Doctor led Kate to her favorite window niche where they sat down, while Martin, Paul, and Margaret crowded around them, whimpering and crying.

"Yes, dear children," he said, "the flesh is sorrowful. It will not be subdued. Parting breaks the heart. And yet," he added, "dear Philip, in my spirit I am happy. For my darling is removed from further earthly ills to her heavenly home where there shall be no more weeping or sorrowing. Is it not a glorious comfort, dear Kate?"

Kate nodded tearfully. "Yes, dear Doctor, it fills my heart with a sort of happiness to know our little Madge is safe. These other poor lambs," she sobbed, tears again streaming down her face, "God only knows what life still has in store for them."

Philip Melanchthon went out with bowed head.

Chapter 16

Life was not the same after Madge's death. Her place could not be filled, even by her little sister Margaret. Hans was sent back to school in Torgau in spite of his protest. Luther told Kate it would only make things worse to pamper him.

Each tried to hide his gnawing grief from the other. Night after night Kate, stifling her sobs in her pillow, whispered, "I cannot forget her—my Madge."

To her surprise, he responded, "The power of love is too great! Every day I see the child before me, just as when she was with us. Every tender word, every loving look of hers rests deep in my heart. I cannot forget."

"Her sunny smile," Kate recounted, "her sweet disposition, her loving-kindness . . ." she could not go on. They sniffed in silent grief for a few moments. Then her Doctor said in a firm voice, "Kate, we should praise our Lord Jesus Christ for having taken her. We know not what evil times she has escaped. Wars already threaten and the Turk is ever a great danger."

Strangely then, peace flooded Kate's heart and she dried

her tears. "Yes, I'm glad she is safe from all that. Who knows what poor little Margaret will have to face?"

"And, after all," he said, "it seems we have no faith to mourn like this. Do we not believe implicitly that one day we will see her again in heaven? Should not that stay our tears?"

It was a quiet Christmas they celebrated this time, and the new year brought no prospect of cheer to Kate. Instead, one day in January, a messenger arrived from Justus Jonas announcing his wife's sudden death. This last blow unnerved Kate completely. Her beloved Katy Jonas dead! She couldn't believe it until they went to the funeral and she saw Katy in her coffin. Then she wept unashamed. Nor could she pretend to be herself for a long time after. For months she went about, lacking the old energy, the old interest in her household. Even Zuelsdorf had not the same attraction. Madge would never again be there. Katy would never be there to cheer her with her gay voice and laughter. And as if this were not enough her Doctor came home one day, a few months later, with unpleasant news for her.

"Kate, I have something to tell you that will not make you happy."

She was sitting in her niche sewing, with the window wide open. Nervously she dropped the cloth in her hand. "Not another death, I hope?"

"No, not that." He cleared his voice and a momentary expression of unhappiness crossed his face. Then he said firmly, "Kate, Justus Jonas is going to marry again."

"What!" she cried, her voice shrill and high. In her

excitement she flung down her sewing and stood up facing him. "Only six months after Katy's death? How can he? He ought to be ashamed of himself! I hate him for that!" She burst into a flood of angry tears.

He let her rage for a moment or two, then he walked up to her and put his hand on her arm. "Kate, you are letting your emotion run away with you."

"I can't help it," she sobbed. "I'm only Katy's friend, but I loved her enough to never forget her. But he—Jonas—her husband, thinks only of getting another woman. If he can be so heartless, I'll be heartless, too," she went on resentfully, "I'll send him no greeting for his wedding."

"Not a gift, either?"

"Never. He'll not get my blessing."

He looked at her sorrowfully. "Kate," he said gently, "you know, I don't approve of his marrying so soon again. But it isn't a sin. There's no law against it."

The old spirit flared up in Kate. She threw back her head proudly. "It's disgracing Katy," she said coldly. "Couldn't he honor her by waiting at least a year?"

"There are small children."

"There are enough women around always that would help a man out."

He shook his head. "You must forgive him, Kate. It's wrong to carry such a grudge. After all, it is his affair, not ours."

Kate did not unbend enough to send a wedding gift. When Grikel visited her in July and they drove out to Zuelsdorf, she told her about it. Grikel, too, was shocked.

But when she said that Agricolas were coming back to Wittenberg to live, Kate thought that the old friendship between the men might be revived. Afterward, when she confided this to her husband, she said, "I don't know why it seemed different. Grikel was nice, and she looks much better than when all those children were small. But . . ."

He nodded. "Once the old charm is broken it can't be recaptured. I can never again feel the same way toward Agricola, though I have fully forgiven him. Besides," he went on, "I have enough physical ailments to make me wish for my heavenly home."

Alarmed she said, "Oh, no, Doctor, not yet. We're just beginning to breathe more freely for the first time since little Madge left us."

His smile was a bit wistful. "We are happier than we have been all these months. Still, with my worn-out old body, my many dizzy spells—stone—old age—I can't expect to live long."

"My dear Doctor," she exclaimed, "you are only going to be sixty in November. That is not 'old age.' Perhaps," she added, "you are very tired again. A visit at Zuelsdorf would stimulate you."

"Not this summer any more," he said seriously, "I'm busy. Far behind in all my work."

"Well then, next year," she coaxed. Solemnly Doctor Luther promised to visit Kate von Bora's old home, Zuelsdorf, in the summer of 1544.

He tried to smile but evidently he was in a very thoughtful mood. "Kate," he began after a while, "I've thought of Wolf, too, in case I go. I talked with him this morning and mentioned Brisger's little house which we bought for him—in case. And the good faithful soul said, 'If you go, then I, too, would wish to die, my father.' "

Kate was moved but also alarmed. "Dear Doctor, is it so bad?"

He groaned and put his hands to his head. "I feel ill. If I'm not better by tomorrow morning, I'll send for Hans. I want him to be with me when the end comes."

"Oh, Doctor!"

"Yes, Kate, I mean it. I'm not imagining. I feel that I will not die suddenly. I'll become sick and lie down. But . . . I will not lie long."

He was better, however, the next morning. Then for a long time there seemed nothing more to worry about. The weeks passed, the first snow, Christmas Eve, New Year's Day, Easter, and Pentecost. Spring came, and summer. This was the year her Doctor had promised to go to Zuelsdorf with Kate. It was such a rare occasion that she took the whole family with her. She could see how restless and absent-minded he was and, for that reason, was glad when he returned to his work in Wittenberg.

During the year that followed, Kate observed changes in him. His hair was turning white. His headaches never entirely left him. He was beginning to feel worn-out and weary. She noticed in him a growing irritation at conditions in Wittenberg. All the old vices against which he had so vigorously preached—gluttony, intemperance, immorality of both sexes, extortion, indifference of the police toward misdemeanors—rankled in his soul. He wrote to Kate from Merseburg where he had gone in

July: "Sell all the property in Wittenberg, Kate, as I am loath to return to that city with its disorderly and immoral doings. Tell Bugenhagen and Melanchthon how I feel about this."

Kate was greatly disturbed at this letter. She conferred with their friends. The University was alarmed. They sent Bugenhagen and Melanchthon to calm him. John Frederick sent his private physician. The theologians sent deputies to him, and the authorities actually made an attempt to suppress corruption. When Luther arrived home about the middle of August, Kate immediately noted his improved appearance. The journey had been good for him. The resentment was gone. Evidently, the men had succeeded in softening him, for he said no more about leaving Wittenberg.

There were other things brewing, however, that gave Kate cause for worry. The quarreling counts of Mansfeld were constantly besieging him to come and help settle their disputes. He wrote letters, trying to put them off and offering suggestions. Kate tried to keep him from brooding over this troublesome affair between the Mansfelds by inviting in cheerful friends. She planned a special dinner for his birthday on the tenth of November with Melanchthon, Bugenhagen, Cruciger, and a few other friends as guests. Although Luther appeared merry, Kate detected a tinge of sadness in everything he said. She sensed that he was thinking of Madge and yearning to join her.

Things did not mend between the two counts. Letters kept coming and, about Christmas, became so urgent that

Kate could find nothing more to say when he decided that he must make the journey to Mansfeld. His beloved Philip would accompany him. This was no comfort to Kate who knew that frail Philip Melanchthon was no fit companion. They started out, but Kate was not in the least surprised when they came back unexpectedly. Philip was put to bed. The man had been ailing, more or less, all his life.

"Perhaps they'll quiet down now," her Doctor had said. "If not, I'll have to go back."

Kate thought the matter would take care of itself. But letters began coming again in January, more imperative than ever. She protested vehemently. "You cannot go, Doctor," she said, "in all this snow and ice and cold. The students tell me that the Saale is frozen solid. As soon as the sun comes out there will be floods."

"You wouldn't want me to turn coward," he said earnestly, "and evade my duty. Besides," he added, brightening, "how about taking the boys with me?"

"All three?" Kate demurred.

"Why, yes. Then I wouldn't be alone. And you know, Kate, how I have always longed to show my sons my homeland."

She nodded bravely. She could see his point. "And their tutor?" she asked. "You will take him, too? And your servant, Franz?"

"Yes, I'll need Franz to look after my things. The boys will have to do some studying, so the tutor goes with them."

On the morning of departure, one of the students casually mentioned hearing a clock fall down on the floor at midnight. Kate started. This was a bad omen. She knew Luther felt the same way when he said, "Do not fear. This means that I shall soon die. And I am weary of this world."

It was a busy morning, with servants running to and fro, the boys carrying and packing their things, the tutor looking after their books, the barber coming in to shave Luther, and Kate supervising everything. Margaret, just entering her twelfth year, was her mother's constant companion. She found little things to do for her father and her three brothers. Melanchthon, with several other professors, came to bid his colleague farewell. Servants, students, friends, and neighbors crowded into the room to see him off.

Tutor Rudtfeldt motioned the boys to get their warm cloaks on. Martin and Paul were impatient to be off on this great adventure. Nineteen-year-old Hans was more sedate. At last the coachman came in to announce that the horses were ready. Luther's servant helped him into his heavy fur-lined cloak, handed him his cap and picked up shawls, blankets, and baggage. Margaret clung to her brothers and took Hans' hand going out. Kate kissed them all, adding a word of admonition to her boys. When she embraced her husband she burst into tears.

"Kate, Kate," he said, patting her arm, "it is God who brings people together and who separates them. It is sad and hurts deeply, but God's will be done."

In a paroxysm of grief Kate wept as they slowly moved out.

"Look, dear Kate," he tried to comfort her, "you are

not left alone—you still have Margaret. And the good Lord is with you always. Have you forgotten 'Come to me, all who labor and are heavy-laden, and I will give you rest?' See," he said gently, as they moved on a few steps, "He will not only help you. No, He will carry you and take the entire burden."

Kate nodded. "My dearest Doctor," she moaned softly, "I am ready to bear all and I know God will help me. But I weep for you. Since you have thought of death so often recently, I, too, can't help feeling so."

He stretched his hand toward heaven. "Kate, you know that our Lord and Saviour has sworn that whoso will keep His Word shall never see death. So let that be your comfort. God will make life everlasting out of death."

She clung to his arm as they approached the carriage where the sons, the tutor, the servant, and others stood waiting. The coachman was growing impatient and the horses stamped their feet, eager to be off. The wind blew coldly around them.

As he held her close and kissed her, he said cheerily, "If we live, we live to the Lord, and if we die, we die to the Lord, so then, whether we live or whether we die, we are the Lord's."

He kissed Margaret once more and called a farewell to Wolf, who was moving about with lagging steps, Toelpel at his heels. Then they were off at a gallop. Kate gazed after the disappearing vehicle, took Margaret's hand, and slowly returned to the house. "It is the end," she whispered when she knew herself to be alone. "I know I shall never again see him alive."

She had not long to wait for a letter. The first, dated January 25, was written in Halle where he had preached that Sunday. They would be detained for several days because the breaking up of the ice on the Saale was followed by heavy floods. Kate couldn't help remarking to Margaret, "That's exactly what I told your father." Then she read on, "We are staying in Jonas' house and have had some good Torgau beer. Pray, and be good."

From Eisleben he wrote on the first of February, ". . . at the village of Rissdorf, near Eisleben, such a bitter wind pierced my cap at the back of my head that I thought my brain must freeze. But now, my dear, gracious Lady Zuelsdorf, do not worry. I am, thank God, quite well again. But the beautiful ladies here are spoiling me."

Hearing of his cold, Kate sent some of her tried and true remedies, and he chided her in his next letter for being overanxious. He went on to complain that the reconciliation was not progressing as fast as he wished. He "would like to grease his carriage wheels and be off in sheer anger. For I am shocked at the avarice, so ruinous to the soul, which both parties display."

On February 7, he addressed her letter: "To my beloved wife Katherine, Lady Luther, Lady Doctor, Lady of the Pig Market at Wittenberg, my gracious wife bound hand and foot in loving service—Grace and peace in the Lord. Pray, read, dear Kate, the Gospel of St. John and the Small Catechism, of which you once declared that it speaks directly to you in all that it contains. For you worry in God's place, as if he were not almighty and able to create ten Martin Luthers for one old one drowned perhaps in the Saale. Well, God's will be done. Let Master Philip see this letter, for I had no time to write to him. You may comfort yourself with the thought how much I love you, as you know. And Philip will understand it all."

The last letter Kate received was dated February 14, and stated that reconciliation between the brother counts had been effected. "Everybody is now happy," he wrote. "There is much mummery and the young folks of both families make merry, go sleighing with bells and dancing and rejoicing all around. Therefore, it must be seen that God is the one who hears our prayers. We hope to return home this week, if God wills." With the letter he sent some trout "as a thank offering from Countess Albert."

Kate sat back with a relieved sigh as she finished the last letter. "Then he will be home soon," she remarked to her daughter. "Oh, thank God, dear Margaret. And don't forget—in every letter he says 'pray, pray, pray.'"

"I do, Mother," Margaret earnestly assured her. "I do pray all the time."

"Five letters in fourteen days," Kate said, fondly holding them close, "when he was so busy all the time, and not feeling well most of the time. Think, Margaret, he preached four sermons, administered Communion twice, and ordained two clergymen."

"And he was sick at Rissdorf," Margaret recounted. "Wasn't that where those armored horsemen and the counts met him?"

Kate referred to one of the letters and nodded. "Perhaps by Saturday," she smiled hopefully, "Father and the boys will be home. Today, you know, is Thursday."

She was unprepared when, on the next morning at six o'clock while the household was at breakfast, there arrived a delegation of friends—Bugenhagen, Melanchthon, Cruciger, Jonas—at the cloister. One look at their faces, and Kate knew. Her premonition had proved true. Her Doctor was dead. She had not been there to perform the last service of love.

Kate listened quietly to the recounting of her husband's last days. Jonas, who had been with him almost constantly during his entire journey, did most of the talking. As Kate looked at him and remembered the unkind feeling she had held toward him ever since his second marriage, she felt ashamed.

"Yes," Jonas related, "he was ill at Rissdorf, as you know. And he was grateful for the remedies you sent him. He labored incessantly for a reconciliation between the counts. He had a feeling that he would remain there at Eisleben where he was born." He paused a moment to give Kate a chance to dry her eyes.

"Did he suffer much pain?" she asked.

"The last evening," Jonas resumed, "he was in pain before supper. So they rubbed him with warm cloths and he joined the party at the supper table, for he said there was no pleasure in being alone."

Kate smiled. "That sounds like the Doctor."

"And," Jonas went on, "he was his own merry self and talked a great deal—jovial and serious, intellectual and pious. Then he returned to his room, stood at the window praying as usual, becoming very uneasy and anxious. Again they rubbed his chest with warm cloths and Count

Albert brought him a special medicine. He went to sleep on the leather couch and slept for an hour and a half. When he awoke he said in Latin, 'Into Thy hands I commend my spirit, for Thou hast redeemed me, Thou God of truth.' "

"You were with him then, too?" Kate struggled hard not to give way to her grief. "Were his sons there?"

Jonas said, "Yes, I was there. Martin and Paul were with him all night. Hans had not yet come back from visiting his relatives. The servant helped him to bed in the adjoining room, and he slept quietly till one o'clock. Then he awoke and asked Franz to heat the room, which was already warm. He came up to me and exclaimed, 'O Lord God, how ill I am! Ah! I feel I shall remain here at Eisleben where I was born and baptized.' "

Kate couldn't suppress a sob, and Margaret, who had come in, stood beside her mother's chair crying. Melanchthon, too, was weeping.

Jonas continued. "He left his bed, then, paced up and down the room once, lay down again on the couch, complaining of the oppression in his chest. Colius, the court preacher, and a young theologian, John Aurifaber, hurried over. Then came the town clerk and his wife, two physicians, Count Albert and his wife, and Count and Countess of Schwarzburg. All these tried to do something to relieve his pain and anguish."

"Oh, God," Kate cried, "that I could not be with him then!"

"They rubbed him and applied warm cloths and when he began to sweat, they thought it a good sign. But he said, 'It is the cold sweat of death. I shall yield up my spirit.' Then he began aloud to thank God for having brought him to the knowledge of his dear Son and cried, 'Into Thy hands I commend my spirit.' Three times he said, 'God so loved the world that he gave his only Son, that whoever believes in him should not perish, but have eternal life.' Colius gave him another spoonful of medicine, and he said, 'I am going, and shall render up my spirit.' And again in Latin he repeated three times, 'Father, into Thy hands I commend my spirit, for Thou hast redeemed me, O Lord God of truth.' Then he lay still with closed eyes, not answering those who were busy with restoratives."

Jonas paused to breathe deeply. Kate sat still with bowed head. Margaret was still crying, her arm locked in her mother's. Wolf and some of the servants who had come to listen were weeping unrestrainedly. Bugenhagen blew his nose. Cruciger sniffed. Jonas brushed his eyes with his hand before going on.

"They rubbed his pulse with strengthening waters and Colius and I asked, 'Reverend Father, will you stand by Christ and the doctrine you have preached?' He replied, 'Yes,' turned on his side and fell asleep. After about fifteen minutes, when his feet were beginning to get cold, he took one deep, even breath. And then his soul was gone."

"When was that?" Kate asked.

Bugenhagen replied, "That was Thursday morning, between two and three o'clock. The eighteenth of February."

Kate looked at the men for further explanation. Cruciger then went on, "They put a white garment on him and laid him in a lead coffin. Hundreds of people came to pay their last respects. Several artists painted his face. The counts had him brought to St. Andrew's Church, where Jonas preached a sermon one day and Colius the following day. Then started the procession for Wittenberg, with a troop of fifty light-armored cavalry in the lead."

"It was most impressive," Jonas went on, "with all the counts and countesses and their guests, the magistrates, the school children, and the whole population following. Everywhere bells tolled. Everywhere people were in mourning. The procession halted at Halle while we came on ahead."

Kate forced herself to be strong. "When will they reach Wittenberg?" she asked. "And what about my sons?"

Bugenhagen spoke, "Your sons are with the procession which is expected to get here in a day or two. You are to hold yourself in readiness with your daughter to be first, after the coffin, in the funeral train, which is to proceed the length of the town to the Castle Church."

Kate swallowed hard. She could see that she was not going to have a word to say about it all. She wished that her Doctor might be buried in the local cemetery beside his two daughters. But she hardly dared ask, for fear of interfering with plans already made.

"Then," she began hesitantly, "he will be . . ."

"He will be laid to rest in the Castle Church," Bugenhagen informed her. "That is what the Elector has decreed."

All Kate could do was to acquiesce.

Chapter 17

The shock of her husband's death and the strain of the funeral proved too much for Kate. She broke down completely. Unable to control herself outwardly any longer, as she at first had done, she withdrew to her room.

For three weeks she suffered the agony of shattered nerves. She was too ill to face the world. Margaret's love and companionship were her greatest comfort. Faithful old Hannah brought her meals and tried to coax her back to normal living. Her sons peeped in, but Kate's weakness was so great that even to speak to them was too much of an effort. To her sister-in-law she wrote, "I am so sad that I can tell my deep sorrow to no one. I don't know how it is—I can neither eat nor sleep. When I think of this beloved, precious man who is lost not only to me but to the entire world, I cannot cease from crying. I can neither read nor write, as you can see by my blurred words."

Among the many letters and messages she received, the one from Jerome Betzold, a onetime student-boarder, touched her most. She and Margaret read it over and over. "My grief grows," he wrote, "by thinking of the very sweetest life with him, who was so full of friendliness and fatherly good will. Never will I let this time of my life get out of my heart . . ." She let the sheet slide from her fingers and remarked to Margaret, "There is one who really appreciated your father."

"Yes, Mother. But there are ever so many others, too."

Kate shook her head sadly. "Somehow I have to think of what Dr. Schurf once told me: 'If they can forget Christ, then they will also forget Luther.' I can feel that they are forgetting him already. No one wants to bother with his widow and children."

Margaret came to her mother's chair, bent down, kissed her gently, and stroked her face. "Mother," she said, "do you remember that countess or princess—wasn't her name Elizabeth—the one you nursed back to health that time?"

Kate nodded slowly. "Yes, child. She was in such great sadness."

"Just as you are now, Mother," Margaret said earnestly. "And I'm going to nurse you back to health as you did her."

Kate's eyes brimmed over. It seemed to her as if Margaret had suddenly grown into young womanhood. "You dear child," she murmured, "God will bless you. But . . ." wearily, "perhaps you ought to go now and get some air, and send Hans up here. He ought to stand by me."

Margaret went and, after what seemed like a long time Hans came in. He kissed his mother lightly, then sat down. "I'm glad you let me come, Mother," he began, "because it's time somebody did something."

"What do you mean?" she asked, not altogether pleased at the manner of his approach.

"Well, what about Father's will? Didn't he make a will?"

Kate felt a twinge of sadness. Had she expected too much from her eldest? After all, he was only going to be twenty in June. "Yes," she murmured, "Father did make a will. I've been hoping to hear from the Elector. I wrote him a letter, but felt too ill to do more."

Hans moved uneasily in his chair. "Well, Mother," he said, "I'm afraid they'll get you out pretty soon."

"I know that. And I'm praying for strength to face things. There will be important matters to settle. Perhaps next week."

Hans rose. "If they try to tell you what to do with your sons," he said, "tell them that I want to go on studying."

"Naturally."

He came forward, kissed her awkwardly, and moved toward the door. "Don't mind if they talk," he called back to her as he closed the door behind him.

"If—they—talk?" Kate repeated, puzzled. What could the boy have meant? She made up her mind at that moment that it was time to crawl out of her retirement and face the world. If they talk, she thought, calling upon all her old determination and iron will, she would talk back.

And that was just what they did—talk! For the Elector was finally moved to sanction her Doctor's will although he complained that it was not drawn up according to the law. When he needed executors and asked Melanchthon and Cruciger to serve as such they declined because "the woman (Kate) does not obey and she would make it difficult for us with her talk." This pained deeply, especially when Kate reflected that they had been almost daily guests at the Black Cloister, and honored guests at her Doctor's last birthday dinner in November.

She sensed that the Elector had been influenced against her. Though he was kind, there was a difference in the way he spoke to her. If he felt that way and Cruciger and Melanchthon refused to be executors, no wonder Katherine Melanchthon was so aloof. Kate now remembered that she had complained to her Doctor about Katherine's strange behavior. He, however, had put her off with a joke. But now, suddenly, Kate knew what was at the bottom of it all: her aristocratic ancestry. Hadn't she heard enough criticism about her pride? Katherine Melanchthon's father had belonged to the rich *bourgeoisie* which many considered above poor aristocracy. She resented Kate's "superiority."

No wonder Hans was so hesitant about telling his mother what he had heard among the students. But she had forced him to say it: "Mrs. Luther is the proudest of all the professor's wives." Didn't she, herself, know that she had this failing, and had she not striven against it for years? She knew only too well that it was this pride, this aristocratic strain in her that had always antagonized Chancellor Brueck. He had opposed her and tried to prevent her from buying Zuelsdorf and the special gardens. Only last winter, Kate remembered, his opposition to her buying the small estate, Wachsdorf, had thoroughly disgusted her Doctor. He had been very angry at Brueck's tactics.

Now, dependent only on herself, Kate braced herself inwardly against storms to come. She was prepared to fight for her rights. She would take up the battle against the Chancellor singlehanded, although she had been told by her brother who had been appointed one of the executors for the will what Brueck had said, "It is Luther's rib—that Kate—that always incites him. She's at the bottom of it all. She is grasping, proud, domineering, selfish, and greedy." Kate couldn't suppress a disdainful smile. Coming from the Chancellor who had hounded her all these years, this did not too greatly affect her. But when she heard what Bugenhagen, one of their oldest and most trusted friends had said, it cut deeply. When the question of the small Wachsdorf property came up, he rapped out, "Now you can see who it is that always strives for property. Before this, the blame was always put on the Doctor. Now it is plain who was at the bottom of it." Reflecting on all that had come to her ears during this short time—especially sharp things said by lifelong friends—Kate remembered her Doctor's words about life being unkind to a woman left alone. How true it was! Yet it did not weaken her. She had won one battle, that of her Doctor's will, and she would win others.

The question of Wachsdorf was next on the docket. Kate pointed out how her husband had tried for over a year to get possession of it, but failed. Brueck expressed himself as vehemently opposed to it. He insisted that Kate "only wanted to rule. She would marry again and enjoy it with a new husband." In order to forestall her getting it, he suggested buying it for her children. For then, he seemed to reason, she would lose interest in it. When Kate gladly agreed to this, the estate became the possession of her four children.

Brueck next opposed her staying in the Black Cloister. "Why all this big household," he ranted, "this unnecessary expense, these many servants?"

Kate forced herself to remain calm while he went on, "The boys should be put somewhere, with some families, so that there need no longer be that expense for so many tutors."

"So many tutors?" Kate repeated, her voice trembling. Such an untruth! And such an imposition—to take her sons from her. She tried to hold her voice down to a calm level as she said, "Rudtfeldt is the only tutor my sons have. And what is more, Chancellor Brueck, I will never give up my sons to anyone. They are not to be bandied about like cattle."

For a moment Brueck seemed checked. But undaunted, he came back to the Black Cloister. "If you and Margaret were alone," he insisted, "your little house, here in Wittenberg, would just be right for you. Then all the rooms in the Black Cloister could be rented, giving you an income. With the gardens and Zuelsdorf you would be well taken care of." He rose to go, saying, "I shall get in touch with the Elector at once. If he will furnish a load of wood and some grain . . ."

"No, no," Kate protested. "I want to stay here and keep my children with me."

But he would listen to no more. Kate knew that he would persuade the Elector to carry out his plan, which sounded reasonable, unless she could forestall his actions. Following an impulse she went to one of the executors, whom she knew and trusted implicitly, and requested him to write a letter to the Elector explaining things from her point of view. Hans, she said, had asked to keep on with his studies which was entirely in accordance with his father's wishes. Paul and Martin had been examined by their tutor Rudtfeldt (not *tutors,* she emphasized) and were doing fairly well. But Martin was sickly and Paul very young. She begged the Elector not to take the boys away from her, because they might more easily get into bad company away from home than if they stayed with her. Also, the executors had promised to supervise their studies.

Kate heard nothing for about a month. Then, one day, the executor came with the joyful news of victory. The battle had been hard-fought. Brueck had tried everything to influence the Elector against her and, for a while, it seemed he would be successful. Finally, the Elector had made this decision: Hans was to continue studying in Torgau, then go on to Koenigsberg; the two younger boys were to stay with their mother and continue with their tutor. All were to be "trained in virtue, hard study, good manners," and so on and "not given much time for pleasuring." Kate was further made happy to hear that she was to go on living in the cloister as before, boarding students.

Soon after this, too, Kate had a message from the King of Denmark, promising to continue his yearly allowance of fifty dollars as he had done previously. She breathed anew. Things were beginning to look better. Had it not been for the insinuations by her Doctor's closest friends, Melanchthon, Bugenhagen, and Cruciger, she might have felt a certain degree of contentment. Tired out, she was anxious for a respite. Hans had returned to Torgau. The two boys and Margaret were under Rudtfeldt's tutorage. The household was normal once again. But disquieting news came from various sources. She remembered things said by her Doctor, from time to time, about the possibility of war. Now, unexpectedly in June, Charles V declared war against the Protestants and the Smalcaldic War was on. Not only that, but the armies actually began moving upon Wittenberg.

At first Kate tried to take things calmly. She worked the gardens as usual while, all around her, people were uncertain. The fear of war hindered every activity. Soon students began fleeing. Instructors followed. Gardens were being destroyed by official order so that they might become a hindrance to the enemy. By October, Wittenberg was no longer safe. Kate fled to Magdeburg with her children, leaving the cloister in the care of faithful Wolf. For the next three months her little family led a hand-to-mouth existence. In January they returned to the cloister, having been told the city was safe. Conditions, however, were unsettled. Kate planned and began to dig and seed some of her garden plots, most of which had been destroyed the year before. But she lacked her former ambition and, when danger approached again in April, she fled a second time.

"If we could only get to Denmark," she complained to her children, "then we would be safe and the good king would help us."

"I like it here in Magdeburg," Martin said.

"But we have no home here," Paul objected. "We can't study. And we don't know where we'll go the next day."

Kate said, "It's bad for you children to live like this. I wonder what the other professors are doing."

"Master Melanchthon is here," Margaret said. "Perhaps he could help us."

The very idea of seeing Melanchthon was distasteful to Kate. For the sake of the children, however, she was willing to swallow her pride and forget his stinging words. She went to him the following day and put her plight before him. "If we would only get to Denmark," she sighed.

He shook his head. "It's impossible," he explained, "you could only get as far as Brunswick. Beyond that, travel is dangerous. All the highways are blocked with soldiers."

This was unexpected news. Kate broke into tears. Master Philip put his hand on her shoulder. "Are you in need?" he asked in his old gentle way.

Kate swallowed hard. "We have no income," she admitted. "We are miserably poor. And were it not for the good woman who has taken us in, we would have no shelter."

He nodded understandingly. "Would a little loan help?" he asked tactfully, fumbling in his pocket.

"Yes, very much," she brightened. "And as soon as times get better, I'll return it. It is so strange here," she murmured softly, "no one knows us or offers to help us. No one remembers the work of Martin Luther."

"That is the way of the world," Melanchthon tried to console her. "It has always been so." He looked thoughtful, then suggested, "If you wish, I shall write to Bugenhagen in Wittenberg to let you know as soon as it is possible for you to return to your home."

Kate was deeply affected. "Oh, thank you so much, dear Master Philip. Then you think there is a chance of returning?"

"The trouble will be over soon, to my way of thinking."

Kate returned to her children with the hopeful news. They had not too long to wait. At the end of June there came a letter from Bugenhagen, stating that the war was over. Wittenberg had new rulers, but she could return to the cloister now, which remained unharmed. At the end he added, "Wolf you will not see again, for he died on the fourth of June."

Kate lost no time returning. Wolf was gone, her gardens were ruined, her cattle had perished, and she had no money. Energetically she set to work once more renting the many rooms and taking in boarders again. Now she even rented the lecture-rooms.

"But there is no money for rebuilding and seeding my land," she lamented. "And my friends have done me more harm than my enemies."

Things began to pick up, however, after a few months of routine life. Two years went by without further calamities. The only thing that troubled Kate was anxiety about Hans. During the two years he had been at school in Koenigsberg he had not written once. Kate had been hurt, puzzled, and angered at her son's behavior. Could a son forget his mother so readily? Now, when he came home with a fairly good certificate, with prospects of becoming Elector John's chancellor at Weimar, and plans of marrying a daughter of Kaspar Kreutziger soon, Kate was moved to forgive. When he left, however, she felt more than ever that her eldest was lost to her.

Martin, too, was still a worry for Kate. He was sickly and, although preparing for the ministry, he would probably never enter the profession. At eighteen, he was sallow and listless.

Paul and Margaret were her stand-bys. Paul was brilliant and she became increasingly proud of him. He was also dutiful and affectionate. He was studying medicine. Kate never doubted that he would some day be an elector's or a king's physician. She expected great things from Paul. The fact that he secretly loved the daughter of a vice-chancellor in Torgau and had told his mother that he would never marry another woman was pleasing to Kate. She wished that he might see the girl more often, for she exerted a wholesome influence on him.

Margaret was Kate's great comfort. What would she ever have done without Margaret during those first trying months of widowhood? Those years with their yearning grief, the fight for her rights and for her own children, the deep disappointment in her closest friends, the alarm of war and the flight from home, misery and poverty, the cold, unsympathetic behavior of people who had received benefits from her husband—all these had bowed Kate's high heart and impaired her health.

But always it had been Margaret—unassuming, grave, gentle Margaret, now seventeen—who had stood by her. She had none of the exquisite charm that had been Madeline's. She was too modest even to compare herself with her sister. Yet, Kate thought, if ever a daughter had been an angel to her mother, it was Margaret, who now cheered her about her swiftly graying hair, her fading strength, and advancing years. "After all, Mother," she said, as they both sat sewing in the old niche, "it wouldn't be natural if your hair didn't turn gray."

"I suppose so," Kate agreed unhappily. "If I could only work as I used to do, I wouldn't mind it so much."

"But you've worked too hard all your life," Margaret replied. "And think what you've been through all these last five years since Father's death."

Kate sighed deeply. "Five years," she repeated slowly. "To me it seems like twenty. And yet I'm not really old. Am I, Margaret?"

"Old?" Margaret laughed in her serious way. "You're only fifty-two. No wonder Chancellor Brueck was so sure you'd marry again."

"Don't remind me of him, child. Thank God for the good Elector, who helped me keep my children together."

"And these last few years," Margaret reminded her, "things have been going pretty well. Our little Paul will be nineteen in January."

"And already he is so deeply in love that I don't know what to do about it."

"Don't do anything, Mother. Paul knows his own mind. He'll marry this girl or no one. And soon, I think."

"I hope he waits until he's twenty-one, at least."

Margaret changed the subject by suggesting that they celebrate Martin's twentieth birthday in November.

"And yours," Kate added, "in December."

"And Paul's and yours together, Mother, in January. We haven't celebrated a birthday for five years."

Kate was fifty-three on the twenty-ninth and Paul nineteen on the twenty-eighth. Margaret arranged things so that the girl Paul loved was present at the celebration. Kate admitted to Margaret that she was pleased with her son's choice. Since he was progressing so rapidly with his studies she saw no reason why marriage plans should not be mentioned within the family. Another year would slip by without anyone being ready for it.

Before many months had passed, however, an old demon reared his head in Wittenberg. In June, the plague set in. Kate, remembering her husband's devout faith and his trust in God's protection withstood it for several months. When the plague entered the Black Cloister in September, her courage failed her. She packed her bags, had the horses hitched up, and started off for Torgau with her two sons and daughter.

Paul was driving, with Martin sitting beside him. Kate and her daughter sat in the rear seat. They had gone about halfway when an odd-looking covered wagon was seen to approach. In nervous fear Kate screamed, "Look out, Paul, the horses are going to shy!"

Paul tried to tighten the reins, but as the clumsy vehicle squeaked by, the frisky beasts took a big jump to the side and went into a gallop. Panic-stricken, thinking only of saving her children, Kate sprang from the wagon just as they were crossing a creek. She plunged into the cold water headfirst. The driver of the clumsy wagon, who had seen everything, hastened to pull her out. By that time Paul had succeeded in quieting the horses and tying them to a near-by tree. All three children ran to their mother's assistance and, wrapping her in blankets, hurriedly carried her back to the wagon and drove on.

The shock and the aftereffects of the dousing in the cold water brought on a heavy chest cold. Noticeably weakened, unable to leave her bed for long, Kate slowly wasted away. Day after day her strength failed her. She deeply appreciated Margaret's loving care and her sons' concern. One day, while having a respite from pain, she began to talk.

"Margaret, I can feel that I'm going."

When Margaret patted her arm and tried gently to hush her, she went on just the same, "You know about the gardens and Zuelsdorf—they were all destroyed in the war. Let them be lost. But Wachsdorf belongs to you four children. And the cloister—that will go back to the Elector." The exertion made her cough and sigh, but she went on determinedly, "What's in the cloister is yours—divide it!"

"Mother!"

"No, child, don't stop me. Your father always said, 'God will provide.' And I know He will, Margaret. A good husband for you and a good wife for Martin. Hans and Paul have already made their choice."

She lay back exhausted, with closed eyes. "Dear Lord God," she murmured, "may it be Thy heavenly will to grant me an early end and a good death. Lord Jesus, I thank Thee for comforting me in my pain and anguish . . ." her voice trailed off weakly.

Again she prayed for the church, for the maintenance of the pure Word of God as her husband had so faithfully taught it. "Oh, that generations in the future may never lose this precious Word of God," was her daily prayer, "this knowledge of the Saviour."

In this way she lingered on patiently, with no complaining, through all of October, November, and part of December.

Then, one day, she called Margaret, asking her to notify the boys. She felt that the end was near. The three brothers came—Hans, with his matter-of-fact manner; Martin, burdened with his own ailments; Paul, young, strong, brilliant, tenderly concerned. And Margaret, weeping quietly.

They heard their mother murmur, "Children, keep strong in faith. Stay with the Saviour . . ." When she paused, they listened tensely. They heard no breathing, no last gasp. But it was over. Her valiant soul had taken flight.

They buried Kate the following day with all the honor and pomp that would once have delighted her. Her body was escorted to old St. Mary's Church in Torgau—the same church in which young Kate on that Easter morning nearly thirty years before, had sung so exuberantly:

Christ is arisen
From the grave's dark prison.
We now rejoice with gladness,
Christ will end all sadness—
Hallelujah! Hallelujah!

Type used in this book
Body, 12 on 14 and 10 on 11 Garamond
Display, Garamond